Lost culture between Kyzylkum and Karakum

By:
Saparbaeva Aziza

© Taemeer Publications LLC
Lost culture between Kyzylkum and Karakum
by: Saparbaeva Aziza
Edition: August '2023
Publisher:
Taemeer Publications LLC (Michigan, USA / Hyderabad, India)

© Taemeer Publications

Book   : *Lost culture between Kyzylkum and Karakum*
Author   : Saparbaeva Aziza
Publisher   : Taemeer Publications
Year   : '2023
Pages   : 80
Title Design : *Taemeer Web Design*

About the Book

It is known that the results of our ancestors who lived in the historical and geographical regions of ancient Uzbekistan, using natural resources, irrigated farming, handicrafts, urban planning and creating the foundations of statehood, made a worthy contribution to the enrichment of the treasure of world culture. One of these ancient historical and cultural regions is Khorezm. The historical period, which had different names in written sources at its various stages, the victories achieved by our ancestors in all spheres of society, were reflected in their content and essence, material and spiritual cultures. This book is dedicated to the history of the hardworking inhabitants of Khorezm, rich in legends, who created a high culture in ancient times.

Responsible editor: Prof. Assoc. Sobirov Qurbanboy

Saparbaeva Aziza was born on May 13, 2003 in Khanka district. In 2021, she graduated from school No. 5 in Khanka district with a gold medal. In September 2021, she was accepted as a student at the Faculty of History of UrSU on the basis of the state budget. Currently, she is a gifted student of the 2nd stage of the university. She is a participant of several international and national conferences. She is the winner and prize-winner of a number of international and republican contests and festivals. About 10 scientific articles and theses by her have been published in republican journals. She is a member of about 10 international organizations.

Review

Khorezm, which has the appearance of a small island due to the influence of the surrounding deserts, is one of the oldest cultural centers of Uzbekistan. The publications of Khorezm archeological-ethnological expedition staff noted that our ancestors, who got used to the vagaries of nature and the vagaries of the Amudarya in this holy land, created a high culture in the historical period and its various stages based on a sedentary life, made a worthy contribution to the development of Central Asian and world culture known from historical information.

Nowadays, when the struggle of different views and ideas is reflected on the world scale, it is important to preserve the objects of cultural heritage, which are the harmony of life and creativity of our ancestors, to pass them on to the future generations, and at the same time to study them. In this sense, the scientific-creative path of Aziza Saparbaeva, who considered it her duty to study the historical path and accumulated experience of the inhabitants of the oasis, is worthy of praise. In the pamphlet, A. Saparbaeva tried to shed light on the unique geographical features of the Khorezm oasis, its differentiation from the processes that took place in the main agricultural oasis of Uzbekistan through Kyzylkum and Karakum, the history of material and spiritual culture specific to the local characteristics, and in finding a scientific solution to this issue, archaeological literature and managed to harmonize the information of written sources. A reader, as a scientist, concluded in the content of the brochure that the knowledge of construction carried out by the population in ancient times was faithful to Zoroastrian wisdom, and as a result of cooperation with the nomadic population, the achievements achieved in all areas of society found their meaning. The information, the author's opinion and comments will be welcomed by the readers without a doubt. At the same time, the information reflecting the content of the brochure will undoubtedly invite young people to study the history of the country.

Reviewer: Assoc. Prof. Sobirov Q.

Contents

Introduction..8

CHAPTER I History of the ancient land between Kyzylkum and Karakum

1.1   Stages of settlement of our ancestors who created a unique culture from the gift of Amu Darya.. 10

1.2   Hunters and gatherers farm training..........................22

CHAPTER II The kingdom of the ancient state of Khorezm

2.1 The history of our ancestors reflected in legends.............30

2.2 Secrets of Aqchakhankala and Tuproqkala.....................41

CHAPTER III Religious Beliefs of Khorezm Residents

3.1   Religious   beliefs   of   the   settled   population   and Zoroastrianism..45

3.2 Religious-ideological centers.....................................58

Summary..64

References and applications...66

List of conditional abbreviations....................................75

Appendices..76

Introduction

If you dig Khorezm

Rivers come out from under the earth.

If you dig Khorezm

Bring out worlds from under the earth.

Matnazar Abdulhakim

Khorezm has been mastered by our ancestors since ancient times, they used the natural conditions and material resources of the land and conducted economic activities in return for their labor. Residents of the Khorezm oasis contributed to the prosperity of the oasis with their creativity and hard work.

Dead the geographical position of our country is also unique, and the Amudarya tributaries are like the blood vessels of the oasis, enriching it with its natural resources and giving it life. Even today, the same Amudarya gives its water to the residents of the oasis and forms the basis of their daily activities. Amudarya played an incomparable role in the creation and development of Khorezm civilization. This is clearly proven by the fact that hydro resources lie at the base of the Kaltaminor culture. The fact that Khorezm is geographically located on a plain and is the westernmost region of our republic, and the absence of high mountains around it, has a direct impact on its climate. The climate of the oasis is sharply continental, meaning that summers are dry and hot and winters are dry and cold. At the same time, the proximity of our country to underground water,

The inhabitants of the oasis created unique works of art with their knowledge of agriculture, handicrafts, architecture, visual arts and music and left a great legacy to the generations. These works of art include irrigation structures, forts, pottery, weapons, and jewelry, which were important for that period.

The book contains the geographical location of our country in the ancient times, natural conditions, anthropogenic structure, economic activities of its inhabitants, legends about the history of fortresses, religious beliefs and rituals of the inhabitants of the oasis, information about the history of visual and musical art, the works of scientists. and making good use of researches, works and scientific works related to the history of Khorezm were carefully studied and tried to be explained through critical and analytical comments. I express my gratitude to my teacher Sobirov Qurbanboy, who did not spare his scientific advice and instructions while writing the book, and to our country, my parents, who support me materially and spiritually.

<u>CHAPTER I</u> History of ancient land between Kyzylkum and Karakum.

- ○ **The settlement stages of our ancestors who created a unique culture from the gift of Amudarya.**

The historical period in the Khorezm oasis, located in the north-west of Central Asia, is the gift of the great Amu Darya River, which in its stages made it possible to use natural resources to serve their goals with skill and dexterity. From the earliest times, Amu Darya, which has given its generosity to the present day, with its tributaries to the right and left, formed a basin around the foot of the southeastern coast of the Aral Sea, reminiscent of the Nile[1] Amu Darya divided the oasis into right and left borders for thousands of years, and the diversity of their geographical landscape is reflected on the map. According to geographical literature, Amu Darya flowed in Karakum, divided the Turan plain into two parts, and as a result of its movement, Okcha Darya, Dovdon tributaries became convenient for human settlement. From the 4th-3rd millennium BC, the oasis area was turned into an ethnic space by mankind. S.P.Tolstov introduced the economic culture of the people of this historical period into the science of history "Kalta Minar culture".[1] BC Until the last quarter of the 6th century, in the areas of the lower Amu Darya basin, they carried out economic activities (hunting in semi-basement huts, gathering and "kayr" farming) and made a step forward in material and spiritual culture. From the last quarter of the 6th century BC, a new era began in the fate of our ancestors. Since this historical period, artisans-engineers who have mastered the knowledge of construction within the population have mastered famous areas due to the construction of main canals from Amu Darya to the right and left borders. As a result of this event, the population built towns and cities that differed quantitatively in the beginning, middle, and end of the irrigation facilities, as well as the heights adjacent to the banks of rivers and tributaries.

---

[1] Толстов С.П Древний Хорезм.-М,: МГУ, 1948-С. 65-69.

The first written source is in the Yasht book of the Avesta, "the brave captains of that country make military campaigns, there are meadows and high mountains watered by water. The rivers Ishkat, Paruta, Margiyan, Areya, Gava Sughda and Khorasmiya flow in waves, and there are ships on them."[2] These historical data indicate that great rivers such as Amu Darya and Syr Darya were active. In the work of the Greek historian Herodotus, Amu Darya is mentioned as the Araks, and it is divided into forty branches, and from one of its branches, others form marshes and marshes. Irrigation facilities, forts, ceramics, weapons, and jewelry are evidenced by the occupation of the people who lived here. Historians of the ancient world, Herodotus, who was named after his father, say that people eat fish and wear sealskin... A single branch of the Araks flows through open lands and flows into the Caspian Sea... So, the Caspian Sea is from the west. bordered by the Caucasus, and on the east side it is approached by an endless plain (Hirkan plain). Noting that a part of this vast plain was occupied by the massagets,[3] This sea does not merge with any other sea. The Caspian Sea is separate and has a distance of 15 days in length and 8 days in width when sailing on a ship. Along its western shore lies the Caucasus, one of the highest mountains... Thus, while the Caspian is bounded by the Caucasus on the west, it is bordered by an endless plain on the east. A large part of this place was occupied by the Massagetae, who were intended to be conquered by Cyrus. From the east, it is approached by an endless plain. A large part of this place was occupied by the Massagetae, who were intended to be conquered by Cyrus. From the east, it is approached by an endless plain. A large part of this place was occupied by the Massagetae, who were intended to be conquered by Cyrus.[4] But Herodotus did not come to Central Asia. Of course, he based the information on the works of Hecataeus Miletsky. The Amu Darya is mentioned

---

[2] Пьянков.И.В. Хорасмии Гекатея Милетского// -М,: «Наука», 1972, ВДИ, №2. – С. 14

[3] Геродот. Тарих. IX. 111. 117.

[4] Геродот. IX. I. 204 – 205.

in Strabo's work, "The river Araks, which divides into branches in many places, gives more water to this country than any other river; it flows with all its branches into the northern sea, and is recorded as the conclusion that one of its tributaries flows into the Hyrcanian gulf.[5]Greek historians were unaware of the historical-geographical toponymy of "Okuz" used in their pronunciation of the inhabitants of Central Asia. In the work of Polybius (204-220 BC) it is said that the Apacians lived between the Oxus and the Tanais, the Oxus river flows into the Hyrcanian Sea, and the Tanais flows into the Meotidis. Both rivers are large and navigable[6]noted in his work. It is possible to agree with the opinion that the Oks river took its water to Hyrkan through Uzboy. But Tanais took its water to the Aral Sea. It is not known where the river Meotida is located.

The economic direction, material and spiritual culture of our ancestors who lived in the lower basin of the Amu Darya, the main irrigation facilities and the irrigation networks from the two sides of the Amu Darya, and the villages and towns that rose up on the middle and intermediate coasts and the adjacent lowlands and heights. accurate information about it is recorded in the works of Arab travelers and geographers Istakhri, Al-Maqsadi, Ibn Rusta. Ibn Rusta's work contains important information about the Lower Amu Darya oasis, the zakhkash, swamp, lake complex that represented its delta, the Amu Darya's discharge into the lake, and the southern shores of the island. In the works of Abu Rayhan Beruni, detailed information about the past history of Karakum, Kyzylkum and Amu Darya found its meaning. It is known that our friend noted that "It (Khorezm) must have been a lake at one time, because Jayhun crossed the Khazarian Sea near the city called Balkhan." . It should be remembered that historical and geographical literature published by researchers who studied the geographical structure of the Khorezm oasis and the history of irrigation facilities during the former Shura period contained extensive information

---

[5] Страбон. География. XI. 6. 8.
[6] Полибий. Умумий тарих. X. 6. 48.

on the history of Amu Darya. According to Y.G. Gulomov, a scholar of the history of irrigation of the Khorezm oasis, after the lowland of the Amu Darya Surkhan oasis, it gradually expanded, its width was 25 km near the city of Chorjoi, and in the distance to Darganota and Jigarband, its width was slightly reduced, that is, 10 created km. At the place where Duldul crosses, the width of Amu Darya is reduced to 358 meters. After crossing Duldul, the river widened again, formed several islands, and entered the territory of Tuyamoin. After the Amu Darya Tuyamoin gorge, it continued to expand to the Toshsaka region. The width of the river is slightly reduced when it comes to Toshsoka region. From Toshsoka, the river began to expand to the right and left, entering the Sultan Uwais mountain system. Between the Shaykh Jalil ridge of Karatog and Yumurtog, a river gorge has formed. He passed from Karki to Amul (Chorjoi), from there to Khorezm, near its capital Kat, and continued to Pilkala. On the basis of this water, swamps, thickets and meadows appeared four farsahs below the city of Khorezm. Amu Darya flows directly from Khorezm and goes between Jurjania and Mizdakhon. Jurjania is in the west, Mizdahkon remained in the eastern region. The river passed through the village of Varagdekh and carried its main water towards the Aral Sea.

In the work of Istakhri, Amu Darya "the border monument of Khorezm on the side of Amul (Chorjoi) was recorded as Takhiriya. And Al-Muqaddasiy, the waters of Amu Darya flooded the surroundings of the city of Jurjania. The inhabitants invented planks and poles to turn it to the other side, as a result, Jayhun went to the east. began to flow.[7] After the Khanate of Khiva was colonized by Russia, historical information about the history of villages, cities and Amu Darya was recorded in the works of Russian experts. Russian researchers M.I.Ivanin, A. V. Kaulbars and N. A. Valuable

---

[7] Ғуломов. Я. Ғ. Хоразмнинг суғорилиш тарихи. Тошкент, "Фан", 1959, б. 20 – 24, 197.

information about the history of Amu Darya is recorded in A.Dimo's works.[8]

In the work of D.Arkhangelsky, it was noted that the diversity of the land surface of the Khorezm oasis and the Sarikamish basin is related to the activity of the Amu Darya and its branches.[9] Based on the dynamics of the Amu Darya, the natural climate, geographical environment and anthropogenic landscape formation process of the lower Amu Darya basin is analyzed in the work of L.S. Berg.[10] K. Markov noted in his research that Central Asia may become a landmass.[11]According to V.L.Shults, the Amu Darya water carried an average of 210-270 million tons of various rocks into the Aral Sea every year. Its water has an average of 3740 grams of turbidity per cubic meter. Amu Darya water is rich in minerals such as phosphorus, potassium, and lime, and it is covered with "fertilizer" that gives an average of 1914 kg of income per hectare.[12]In the works of the Khorezm expedition staff, information was recorded about the creation, formation and development of the geographical environment and anthropogenic landscape of the lower Amu Darya, Sarikamishboi and Uzboy lowlands in different geological and historical periods with the movement of the Amu Darya.[13]V.B.Andrianov, an employee of the Khorezm expedition in the Arolboi lowland, paid attention to the activities of networks.[14]

---

[8] Иванин. М. И. Хива и река Амударьи. СПб, 1873, с. 37 − 39. Каульбарс. А. В. Низовья Амударьи, описание по собственным исследованниям в 1873г// ЗИРГО, Т. 3// СПб, 1881. Димо. Н.А. Почвенные исследования в бассейне в Амударьи// Ежеговник отдело земельных улучшений за 1913г. Ч.2, СПб, 1914.

[9] Архангельский. А. Д. Геологические исследования в низовьях Амударьи. Москва, 1931, с. 39.

[10] Берг. Л.С. Климат и жизнь. М, 1947.

[11] Марков. К. К. Высыхаетли Средняя и Центральная Азия// Очерки по географии четвертичного периода//. Москва, 1955.

[12] Баратов. П. Ўзбекистон табиий географияси. Тошкент, " Ўқитувчи", 1996, б 80 - 82

[13] Низовья Амударьи, Сарыкамыш, Узбой//История формирования и заселения//. МХЭ, Вып, №3,М, «Наука», 1960.

[14] Андринов. Б. В. Древние оросительные системи Приаралья. М, «Наука», 1969.

According to the researchers, 4-3 million years ago, a wide lowland was formed in place of the Aral-Sarikamish depression.[15]According to the results of II Gerasimov's research, at the beginning of the lower and middle Quaternary periods of the earth's geological period, the Amu Darya flowed westward to the Caspian Sea from the vicinity of Chorjui.[16]According to II Gerasimov, the Arolboi, lower Amu Darya, and Sarikamish lowlands are made up of deserts.[17]

According to the work of the geographer P. Baratov, at the beginning of the Quaternary period of the earth's geology, the Amu Darya Surkhan lowland, covering the waters of the Vrevskii glacier at an altitude of 4950 meters on the northern slope of the Hindu Kush mountain, began to serve human interests. The Amu Darya water turns westward from Kelif, and after the city of Karki in Turkmenistan, through Kelkor and Aktam in the north of Ungizi Karakum, covers the waters of five tributaries of the Zerafshan river, Kashkadarya, Guzordarya, and flows to the Caspian Sea through a 550-kilometer corridor, forming the southwestern lowland of Ungizi Karakum. was.[18] This lowland is known as Uzboy in geological and geographical literature. The scenery of the Uzboy lowland is described by Kangkakir, Tuzkir, Tarimkiya, which have a height of 80-100 m. In the 3rd millennium BC, there was a water flow in Uzboy, but in the 2nd millennium BC, water activity stopped on this border.

In the middle of the Quaternary geological period, due to the deposition of turbidity layers in the water of the Dovon

---

[15]Виноградов. А. В.,М.А.Итина, А.С.Кесь. Мамедов. Э.Д.Палеографическая обусловленность расселения древнего челоека в пустыях Средней Азии//Первобытный человек, его материальная культура и природная среда в плейстоцене и голоцене//М, «Наука», 1974, с. 290 – 291.

[16] Герасимов.И.И. Основны черты развития современной Турана//ТИГ.Вып.25//. 1937. с. 63

[17] Герасимов.И.И. Марков.К.К. Четвертичная геология. Москва, 1939, с. 270 – 271.

[18] Баратов. П. Ўзбекистон табиий географияси. Тошкент, " Ўқитувчи", 1996, б. 154 – 162.

tributary over thousands of years, Kopet Dog and its surroundings Uzboy, Ungizi Karakum rise and the Karakum plain and the southern regions of the Aral basin slope.[19]The water basin was created as a result of the activities of the shallow Dovdon tributary, which exists in the vast plain from the north of Karakum to Kokhna Urgench. The Sarikamishboi delta consisted of a lowland. Unguzi Karakum. The lowland near Sarikamishboi and Kokhna Urgench consists of Cretaceous, mostly Tertiary rocks of the geological period.[20] The surface of this border decreases by 0.2-0.4 meters per kilometer from the vicinity of Kokhna Urgench towards the Sarikamish basin, and its area is 1 million hectares. The activities of Dovdon and its tributaries Kangkha Darya and Tunidarya of Amu Darya played an important role in the prosperity of the lowland.[21]As a result of the late Khvalin period, Lake Khorezm was filled with sedimentary rocks from the Amu Darya, and a fertile plain filled with alluvial deposits was formed in its place.[22]

Dovdon is 300 km from the left bank of Amu Darya, and Daryoliq is 250 km. Davdon separated from Khanka and Urgench, and Daryoliq separated from Amu Darya 18 km north of Urgench. Due to the unstable flow of Amu Darya water, the occasional rise of the water flow created several branches, but their movement was not constant. The Dovdon tributary snakes its way to Sarikamishboi, and its branches to the south and west supply the surrounding areas with water. There is a slight difference in the direction of the tributary, that is, it is directed towards Lake Sarikamish, as the Bolkhan Mountains obstructed

---

[19] Баратов. П. Ўзбекистон табиий географияси. Тошкент, " Ўқитувчи", 1996, б. 80 - 82

[20] Архангельский. А. Д. Геологические исследования в низовьях Аму - дарьи. Москва, 1931, с. 39. Ғуломов. Я. Ғ. Хоразмнинг суғорилиш тарихи. Тошкент, "Фан", 1959, б. 39.

[21] Андринов. Б. В. Древние оросительные системи Приаралья. М, «Наука», 1969, с. 146. Низовья Амударьи, Сарыкамыш, Узбой. М, «Наука», 1960, с. 147 – 174.

[22] Низовья Амударьи, Сарыкамыш, Узбой//История и заселения человекам//. М, «Наука», 1960. с. 21.

the flow of water that started from the left bank of the Amu Darya to the west.

Under the influence of the Amu Darya water dynamics, the irrigation facilities released from the Dovdon tributary formed the lowland as a result of the rising and falling of the water flow of the Charmanyob, Manqir, Tunidaryo and Daryoliq tributaries.[23] By the middle and end of the Quaternary period, due to the activities of the Amu Darya's Davdon and Daryoliq tributaries, the colorful anthropogenic landscape and geographical features of the Sarikamishboi basin lowland were finally formed.[24]As a result of the fluctuating flow of the Amu Darya, the direction of the Dovdon and Daryoliq tributaries often changed (currently, information about the passage of the tributary is often found among the residents of Madaniyat, Bogalon farm in the Yangibozor district of the Khorezm region. There is a village called "Ocha" on the border of Qilichboy, located on the side of the river. In this area, two branches of the Daryalyq branched off towards Sarygamysh lake, and a lowland suitable for farming was formed between them, which led to the constant use of the above-mentioned term in the pronunciation of the local population.

Based on the geomorphological structure of the Akchadarya basin lowland, it is divided into southern and northern regions. In the middle of the Quaternary geological period, the Amu Darya entered the Khorezm Lake in the lowland, and the Amu Darya water filled the Okchadarya tributary.[25]In this historical period, the water of Akchadarya flows from the eastern side of the Sultan Uwais mountain to the Kyzylkum desert through the first existing corridors to the northeastern corner of Khorezm Lake, and the second, bounded

---

[23] Низовья Амударьи, Сарыкамыш, Узбой//История формирования и заселения//. МХЭ, Вып, №3,М, «Наука», 1960. с. 16 – 17.

[24] Толстов.С.П., Кесь.А.С. История первобытных поселений на протоках древних дельт Амударьи и Сырдары//Сборник статей для XVIII международного географического конгресса//. М – Л,1956, с. 270 – 271.

[25] Низовья Амударьи, Сарыкамыш, Узбой//История формирования и заселения//. МХЭ, Вып, №3,М, «Наука», 1960, с. 17.

by the Beltov hills, came to the Aral basin from the northeastern side.[26] According to the researchers, during this geological period, the center of Karakum became the "Tentirash" area of Amu Darya.[27]

By the end of the 4th-3rd millennia BC, swamps and water bodies were formed around its shores due to the occasional inflow of water from the Amu Darya Davdan tributary and the saturation of the southern Akchadarya tributary.[28] According to the results of geological studies conducted by the researcher A.S. Kes, the rise of the Amu Darya water level exceeded the coastal rise in 25-22 thousand years ago, and the surrounding area was marked by sand dunes.[29] The Akchadarya tributary on the right bank of the Amu Darya is divided into several branches and directed towards the north. The Okchadarya branch turns from the south of the Sultan Uvais mountain, merges with the eastern Okchadarya, which moves along the northeastern border, breaks through to the north of Kyzylkum, and forms the 75 km long Okchadarya basin. Akchadarya tributary, along its course from the east of Sultan Uvais mountain, to the north vertically in a triangular shape (its length is 170 km), several separate branch waters came to the Aral Sea. So, the southern Akchadarya basin was formed on the border from Shorokhan to Sultan Uwais mountain. The southern and southeastern borders of the basin are connected to Kyzylkum.

The turbidity brought by the Akchadarya every year has created a lowland of 80-150 meters. It consists of shallow depressions, heights and ravines, mountain ranges, dry valleys and lakes, and the dunes connected to them vary in height. From the Middle and Lower Holocene period to the 2nd millennium

---

[26] Низовья Амударьи, Сарыкамыш, Узбой//История формирования и заселения//. МХЭ, Вып, №3,М, «Наука», 1960, с. 20.

[27] Баратов.П., М.Маматқулов., А.Рафиқов. Ўрта Осиё табиий географияси. Тошкент, " Ўқитувчи", 2002, б. 162, жадвал. II.

[28] Ўша асар. 1960, с. 66.

[29] Кесь.А.С. Аральское море в голоцене//Археология и этнография Средней Азии//. Москва, «Наука», 1979, с. 19.

BC, due to the high level of water saturation of the Akchadarya and Dovdon tributaries, Amu Darya water flowed into the Aral Sea in small quantities. According to A.S. Kes, by the 2nd millennium BC, the waters of the Dovdon and Daryalik tributaries of the Amu Darya flowed into the Sarygamysh swamp, and the water supply of the Akchadarya tributary was at a high level.[30] Due to the rise of the water level of this historical Amu Darya river and its bursting into the corridor formed between the sand dunes on the northeastern side of Yonboshkala, a large number of lakes system was formed in the term of Suvyorgan. The area from the Toshsoka Gorge to the Aral Sea is 100 m above sea level. The coast of the Toshsoka border was 8-10 m above the river water level, while the right bank areas were low and 1-3 m above the surrounding land. Due to the low status of these areas, our ancestors who led a lifestyle on the border faced the capricious actions of Amudarya (it is enough to remember the situation of the city of Beruni, Turtkul).[31]

According to the results of geological studies, at the end of the Quaternary period, the eastern Aralboi basin was formed due to the arrival of Jonadaryo, Kuvondarya, and Eskidaryalik tributaries from the left bank of Syr Darya to the north-west.[32] At the end of the first half of the 1st millennium BC, several branches of the Amu Darya branched off from the vicinity of Takhiatash and formed the north-western Aralboi as a result of the direction of their waters. The eastern Aralboi basin was created as a result of the northward direction of the branches of the Oqdarya, Kokhnadarya, Toldiqdarya, Erkindarya, Kazakhdarya, which started near the city of Nukus. In this way, the Aralboi Basin, covering an area of 50 km, was created. According to B.I.Vaynberg, in the second half of the 1st millennium BC, the main water volume of the Amu Darya

---

[30] Кесь.А.С. Аральское море в голоцене//Археология и этнография Средней Азии//. Москва, «Наука», 1979, с. 20.

[31] Андринов. Б. И. Древние оросительные системы Приаралья. М, «Наука», 1969.

[32] Кесь.А.С. Природные факторы, обусловающие расселение древнего человека в пустыне Средней Азии//КСИЭ, Вып XXX//. М, «Наука», 1958, с. 172.

branched off in the eastern region and went to the island.[33] The area of the Aral Sea is 67.34 thousand square meters. km, depth 69 m, average depth 16.1 m.[34] It is noticeable that there are different opinions about the history of the Aral Sea.

L.S.Berg, D.A.Arkhangelsky, B.M.Georgievsky put forward the opinion that the lake was formed as a result of sedimentation under the influence of underground movements on the border of the Aral Sea. I.P. Gerasimov, Y.A. Skvortsov came to the conclusion that the waters of the Western Siberian and Chu rivers formed the bottom of the Aral Sea. A.S. Kes says that the Aral Sea was formed 100 thousand years ago. P.I.Chalov, K.N.Merkulova. Those who came to the opinion that T.V.Tuzova was formed 130-150 thousand years ago. In the study of R. Qurbaniozov, the geological structure of the borders of Sarikamishboi, Uzboy and Aralboi, which formed the Lower Amudarya and its territorial system, was divided into four types. Borders made of ancient crystalline rocks: Yumurtog, Kubatog, Sultan Uwais mountain and Aralboi regions,[35]P. Baratov divided the Sarikamishboi, Uzboy lower Amu Darya borders into natural and geographical zones such as Chimboy - Kungirot, Beltov and Khorezm.[36]

In Uzboy, Okchadarya basin, Tuyamoin environs, and Sarikamishboi borders, around the water basins naturally collected as a result of the movement of Amu Darya water and its rise, under the influence of anthropogenic landscape, a favorable geographical environment and geographical boundaries of natural conditions were formed.[37]

---

[33] Вайнберг.Б.И. Этногеография Турана в древности. М, «Наука», 1999, с. 22.

[34] Баратов.П., М.Маматқулов., А.Рафиқов. Ўрта Осиё табиий географияси. Тошкент, " Ўқитувчи", 2002, б. 119, 283 – 284.

[35] Қурбонниёзов.Р. Хоразм географияси. Урганч, 1996, б – 7.

[36] Баратов. П. Ўзбекистон табиий географияси. Тошкент, " Ўқитувчи", 1996, б. 161 – 162.

[37] Андрианов.Б.В. Земледелия наших предков. М, "Наука", 1978, с. 108 – 110.

Due to the occasional rise in the Amu Darya water level, massifs disappeared around Yonboshkala Hill, while new massifs with an anthropogenic landscape appeared in the southern Okchadarya, Tuyamoin zone, Sarikamishboi and Uzboy watersheds. On this historical date, the northern Okchadarya basin was formed as a result of the joining of the eastern branches of the Okchadarya tributary and the Jonadarya tributary of the Syr Darya. In the North Okchadarya, low-lying water basins were created, and at the foot of its shores, under the influence of anthropogenic landscape, low-lying massifs, which often change, were active.

As the activity of the Dovdon tributary of the Amu Darya continues to rise and fall, the activity of the anthropogenic landscape massifs at the foot of the shores of the reservoirs around the borders of Sarikamishboi and Uzboy has come to an end. In connection with the rise of the Amu Darya water regime, new massifs were formed with the creation of new water bodies around the Akchadarya basin and the Tuyamoin zone. As a result of Amu Darya water rushing towards the range of sand dunes in the northeast of Yonboshkala Hill, a system of lakes was created in the Suyorgan terminus, which is not in constant movement in the lowlands bordered by Kyzylkum. At the foot of the shores of these water bodies and lakes, dense massifs with seasonal anthropogenic landscape were formed.

1.2 Hunters and gatherers farm training.

In Ustyurt chink, which is connected to the northwestern region of the lower Amu Darya basin, the regional geography of the first ethnic areas was created as a result of the human assimilation of the materials taken from the Yesen-2,3, Karakuduq and Churuk-12 areas in the lower Acheulean period.[38] E.B.Bijanov, in the early Ashelian period, around the Shahpakhta Basin, people were hunting, their weapons were stone. It should be noted that the policy of exploitation of primitive hunters was carried out around the Shahpakht basin. According to the researchers, Haydarkon in the south-west of the Fergana Valley and Selengur Cave in the Sokh Valley,[39] Kolbuloq, on the slopes of Chatkal Mountain in the Ohangaron Valley of Tashkent Region, on the coast of Kizilolmasoi,[40] At the foot of the Nurota mountain range, hunters who worked in Uchtut-Ijond and Vaush settlements created a geographical breadth and conducted hunting and gathering.[41]Also, in the mountainous region of South Kazakhstan, Borikazigan, Tanirqizigan, Takali-1,2,3, Kamar and Shabakti-1, Sariarka on the northern, eastern and western borders. Semizbugu, Khudaikul and Aybat, Kyzylkala in Kyrgyzstan, On - Archa,[42] In southern Tajikistan, Karatog-1, Khavalang, Lokhuti, and Tomchisuv in the central part of Turkmenistan, in the area adjacent to the foothills of the eastern shore of the Caspian Sea, the settlements of Yangaja and Karatangir were occupied by

---

[38] Винаградов А.В, Бижанов Е.Б. Первие палеолитические находки с юго – восточнова Устюрта/АО, 1977. –М, Наука, 1978 Бижанов Б.О находках памятники каменного века в районе впадины Шахпахты на Устюрте//Вестник Каракалпакского филиала АН УЗССР.-Нукус,:№1, 1983. – С.65 – 66

[39] Исламов У. Древнейшая перещерная палеолитическая стоянка Селенгур Ферганской долине – СА, 1990, №2. – С. 115-126. Ўша муаллиф. Фарғонанинг ибтидоий тарихи//Анорбоева А, Исломов У, Матбобоев Б Ўзбекистон тарихида қадимги Фарғона-Тошкент, Фан, 2001, -Б. 36

[40] Касымов М,Р. Многослойная палеолитическая стоянка Кульбулак в Узбекистане-МИА, 185, М. 1972. – С. 3-12

[41] Мирсоатов М.Т. Древние шахты Учтута – Ташкент, Фан, 1972. – С. 5-120

[42] Кабиров Ж, Сагдуллаев А.С. Ўрта Осиё археологияси – Ташкент, : Ўқитувчи, 1990. – С. 22

hunters of the Ashele period.[43] As a result, it is possible to create a geography and ethnodemographic cartography of settlements of primitive people and ethnic groups around Shahpakht basin.

Due to the favorable climate and ecology of the Ustyurt region, during the continuation of practical training, the population increased, labor equipment was limited, and the problem of ecology arose. And these, in turn, were forced to carry out the policy of development of neighboring natural and economic areas.

In the north-west and south-west regions of Ustyurt, hunters of the Middle Stone Age continued their ethnic processes due to the favorable climate and ecological situation, while a group of people in the south-east region of the Ustyurt Plateau lived in the Sultan Uwais mountains. He has mastered the territory of the coast. According to AI Vinogradova, the materials obtained as a result of excavations at Burli-3 settlement in the area of Sultan Uwais mountain belong to the last stone age.[44] Based on the results of E.B.Bijanov's research, it can be concluded that the representatives of a group of hunters in the southeastern region of Ustyurt settled in the surroundings of Sultan Uwais mountain in order to continue their practical life experience, and the communication routes leading to blood and kinship were founded. The material objects taken from Burli-3 location can be concluded that ethnic processes in the northern region of Khorezm started from the last stone age.

According to historical data, the hunters of Ustyurt chinki and the foothills of Sultan Uwais mountain carried out their

---

[43] Лазаренко А.А, Ранов В.А. Новая палеолитическая стоянка Каратау-1 в Южном Таджикистане//Успехи среднеазиатской археологи – Л, Наука. Вып-3, 1975, - С. 69-71. Сагдуллаев А.С. Қадимги Ўрта Осиё тарихи – Ташкент, Университет, 2004. –Б. С. 11

[44] Виноградов Е.А. Первие палеолитические находки в\ Султонуиздаге//Приаралъе в древности и средневековье.-М, Наука, 1998, -С. 74-78

daily work and continued the ethnic processes.[45] According to the researcher, the complex of monuments in the area of the Ustyurt plateau belonged to clan communities of the Mesolithic period.[46]

When the ancient stone age came to the Neolithic period, the Mesolithic hunters were the material basis for the development of the economic culture. It reflects the geographical position of the right bank of the Amu Darya. The organic world of water bodies, which are located among the Kyzylkum mounds, reflecting the geographic image of the Yonboshkala area, was a serob. Also, their coastal foothills are thickets and reeds, so our ancestors used to hunt and gather in their daily life. The fishing industry was especially dominant, as 80% of the bones were fish bones.[47]

Ground-level huts were important for Neolithic hunters to sustain their daily activities.[48] In S.P.Tolstov's fundamental work, the mastery of the Akchadarya basin by the clan communities of the Neolithic period, based on the material objects obtained from the cultural layer of the Yonbosh-4 location, the economic culture they carried out in the first Neolithic (the end of the 4th millennium - the beginning of the 3rd millennium, the second one in the 3rd millennium it is noted that it belongs to the middle - the beginning of the II millennium.[49] In the second study of the scientist, he noted that

---

[45] Виноградова А.В. Мамедов Э.Д. Ланшафтно-климатические условия среднеазиатских пустынь в голоцене//ИМКУ-Ташкент, 1974 №11. −С. 32-44

[46] Бижанов Е.Б. Открытые памятники мезолита на юге-восточном Устюрте//Вестник Каракальпакского Филиала АН УЗССР. −Нукус, Вып-3, 1982. −С. 61-65. Ўша муаллиф. Мезолитические и неолитические памятники северо-западного Устюрта//Археология Приаралья. − Ташкент, Вып-1, 1982, -С. 14-38.

[47] Низовья Амударьи, Сарыкамыш, Узбой. История формирование и заселения человекам. - М, МХЭ, Вып-3, 1960.- С.21-25. Баратов П. Маматкулов М., Рафиков А Ўрта Осиё табиий географияси. Тошкент, «Ўқитувчи» 2002, -С. 293

[48] Низовья Амударьи, Сарыкамыш, Узбой. - С. 35-147.

[49] Толстов. С. П. По следам древнехорезмийской цивилизации. - М-Л, 1948. - С.70, Рис.34

the first Neolithic belongs to the end of the IV millennium), and the next to the III-II millennia.[50] S.P.Tolstov managed to place the term "Primitive Khorezm" on the page of world history.[51]

In his first work, A.Vinogradov divided the history of clan communities of Khorezm Neolithic period into early, middle and late periods, that is, he noted the historical date as the boundary of the III-II years, the second half of the IV millennium.[52] In the researcher's monograph, the culture of the seed communities of Central Asian Neolithic communities belonging to the lower Zerafshan Neolithic period (VII-VI millennia) Daryosoy stage, the first stage in the Okchadarya basin Yonbosh - 4 (second half of the IV millennium), the last date is III-II concluded as the end of the millennium.[53] And N. Kholmatov, the history of the Neolithic period is the first Neolithic Daryosoy stage (end of the 7th millennium BC - the middle of the 5th millennium) middle Neolithic (the end of the 5th millennium - the middle of the 4th millennium BC (Yonbosh-4), so. The late Neolithic estimated the historical date of the second half of the 4th millennium - the middle of the 3rd millennium.[54]

In the publications of researchers, it is difficult to observe a single opinion about the origin of the clan communities that have mastered the surroundings of the Yonboshkala Heights. According to historical data, a group of hunters from the eastern coast of the Caspian Sea settled along the coast of Uzbay, in the

---

[50] Толстов. С. П. По древним дельтам Окса и Яксарта. - М, Наука, 1962.- С. 30.

[51] Толстов. С.П. Древнехорезмийские памятники в Каракалпакии (Предварительные итоги археологических работ ИИМК в 1938г//ВДИ, М, Наука, - М, 1939, Вып-3 .-С. 172-199.

[52] Виноградов А.В. Неолитические памятники Хорезма. -МХЭ, М, Наука, 1968, Вып-8. -С.155.

[53] Виноградов А.В. Древние охотники и реболове Среднеазиатского междуречья.- М, Наука, 1981. -С.133-134.

[54] Холматов. Н.Ў. Ўзбекистон неолит даври жамоалари моддий маданияти. - Тошкент, Фан, 2008.-. С. 18-19. Виноградов А.В. Итина М, А, Яблонский Л.Т. Древнейшее население низавий Амударьи- М. Наука, 1986.-С. 7-79. Вайнберг Б.И. Памятники Кююсайской культуры //Кочевники на границах Хорезма//ТР. ХАЭЭ-М, Наука, - М 1979, Т-XI-С. 27. Табл.XVI.

lower Amu Darya basin.[55]M.A.Itina believes that Yonboshlik hunter-gatherers had cultural contacts with the people of the South Urals.[56]The ethnic processes in the Okchadarya basin during the Neolithic period were recorded by the hunters of Sultan Uwais Mountain in the millennium BC. At the end of the 5th millennium - the first half of the 4th millennium, they abandoned their homeland and settled in the vicinity of the Yonboshkala Heights. Taking into account the historical situation in which the "wise mother" appeared in the second half of the 4th to the 3rd millennium BC, the territories of the Tuyamoin and Sarikamishboi basins were developed. Bones from the Tumek-kichidjik tomb left by the inhabitants of Kaskajal on the Ustyurt Plateau, Yonbosh-4 and Yonbosh-5 settlements in the southern Okchadarya basin, and the southwestern Kuyisoy height indicate that the clan carried out ethnic processes in the Late Neolithic period.[57]However, in the publications there is no information about the burial structures of clan communities of Ustyurt chinki, Okchadarya basin, Tuyamoin regions.

The Eneolithic period (the middle of the IV millennium - the first half of the III millennium).

It should be noted that under the influence of the material and spiritual culture created by the clan communities of the Neolithic period, the inhabitants of the Eneolithic period formed the basis for the development of all areas of society. Between Tuyamoin, Shorakhan and Sultan Uwais, descendants of the last Neolithic inhabitants continued their practical experience. According to historical data, in the 4th-3rd millennium BC, the inhabitants of Beleuli-2, Markabay-2, 3 settlements in the northeast of Ustyurt continued ethnic processes.[58]Similar processes

---

[55] Средняя Азия в эпоху камня и бронзы – М -Л, Наука, 1866.-С. 143-144

[56] История степных племен Южного Приаралья// ТР ХАЭЭ-М, Наука, 1977, Т-Х. - С.23-24.

[57] Бижанов Е.Б. Первое неолитическое погребение на Устюрте. - СА, Наука, 1985, Вып-1. -С. 250-252.

[58] Бижанов Е.Б. Новые данные о неолите юго-западногр Устюрта//Вестник Каракалпакского филиала АН Уз ССР.-Нукус, 1980, Вып-3.-С.75

were adopted by the representatives of the population living in the lower basin of the Dovdon tributary at the height of Kuyisoy in the northern and southern regions of Uzboy (Bola-Ishem-8,9, Togolok settlements).[59]The anthropological objects taken from Tumek-kichidjik tomb are used to study the burial customs of the people living in the surroundings of Kuyisoi Heights.[60]Unfortunately, in the works of researchers, there is no information about the burial structures of clan communities that operated in the regions of Tuyamoin and Okchadarya basins. In our opinion, the materials taken from the houses and rooms of the semi-basement settlements with wooden pillars explain the past ethnic processes. In the course of this historical period, the basis of the economy was the exploitative economy (hunting, gathering).

Bronze Age (middle of the III millennium - II millennium).

This period is characterized by certain changes in the economy of the people who lived in settlements on the shores of water bodies. According to historical data, Belkuli-1 in Ustyurt. The residents of Isatoy-3.4, Markabay-3 settlements received handmade ceramics.[61]According to historical data, the people who settled in the foothills of the reservoirs in the Tuyamoin region during the Bronze Age continued ethnic processes.[62]In the works of S.P.Tolstov, M.A.Itina and Y.Gulomov, opinions on the paleogeography and paleoecology of the Bronze Age

---

[59] Толстов С.П. Работы Хорезмской археолого-этнографической экспедиции в 1948-1953//ГРХАЭЭ- М., Наука, 1958, Т-11-С. 66-67. Итина М.А. Работы Узбойского отряда в 1957г//КСИЭ, М. Наука, 1958, Т- ХХУІ, -С. 105-113

[60] Вайнберг Б.И.Памятники К//осайской культуры// Кочевники на границах Хорезма.//ТР ХАЭЭ-М, Наука, 1979, Т.XI, -С. 27. Виноградов А.В. Итина М.А, Яблонский Л.Т.. Древнейшее население низавий Амударьи-М, Наука, 186.-С.7-79

[61] Бижанов Е.Б., Виноградов А.В. Неолитические памятники Каракалпакского Устюрта//Вестник Каракалпакского филиала АН УЗ ССР-Нукус, 1965, №3-С. 65. Ўша муаллиф. Новыие данние о неолита на юге-западного Устюрта//Вестник Каракалпакского Филиала АН УЗ.ССР-Нукус, 1980.№3, -С.75

[62] М.А. Памятники эпохи неолита и бронзк/ревности Южного Хорезма. ТР ХАЭЭ-М, ИВЛ РАН, 1991, Т. XIV -С.73-79.

society and population migration issues are recorded. According to S.P.Tolstov, in the middle and second half of the 2nd millennium BC, representatives of Yogochband and Andronova, who surrounded Central Asia from the northeast to the south of Kazakhstan, came to the southern Akchadarya basin from the southern Urals and western Kazakhstan. settles down and explains the farm he conducted under the name of "Tozabogyob" culture.[63]At the same time, the researcher came to the conclusion that the irrigated tribes carried out ethnic processes from the regions of the Iranian plateau and South Turkmenistan to the Lower Amu Darya basin.[64]Academician Y.G. Gulomov, in his fundamental work, is right that the objects taken from the Yonbosh-6 location reflect the practical experience of the Yonbosh-4 clan communities and explain the migration process of the Tozabogyob.[65]M.A.Itina's work does not contain information about water bodies, but from the middle of the 2nd millennium BC, there is a tribe's economy between the Volgaboi and the Ural Mountains, from the deserts of Yogochband and Kazakhstan, to the region of South Akchadarya. The research that noted that they are representatives of Tozabogyob noted the Amirabad culture on the basis of the Qovunchi culture, which arose as a result of the interbreeding of aquatic animals with Tozabogyob.[66]Y.A.Zadneprovsky, Y.G.Ghulomov's Paying attention to conclusion about the Suvyorgan culture, he doubts that the Suvyorgan culture migrated from the south to Khorezm.[67] H.Matyakubov, who took into account the opinions of Y.G.Gulomov, Y.A.Zadneprovskyi about water peoples, "If the water peoples settled in the south of the Okchadarya basin, they could use clay construction and architectural styles in the

---

[63] Толстов С.П. Древнехорезмийские памятники в Каракалпакии//ВДИ,-М, 1039, №3.-С.174-175.

[64] Толстов.С.П. Древний Хорезм С. 67.

[65] Ғуломов.Я.Г. Хоразмнинг суғорилиш тарихи. -Тошкент, Фан, 1959.-С.54-55.

[68] Итина М.А. История степных племен южного Приаралья //ТР ХАЭЭ-М, Наука, 1977, Т-Х. -С. 47-148.

[69] Заднепровский Ю.А. Памятники Андроновской культуры. К вопросу о сувярганской культуре// Средняя Азия в эпоху камня и бронзы М-Л, Наука, 1966.- С. 213-214.

construction of their settlements. we can agree with the conclusion that they were far from the knowledge of clay construction in the future".[68] In the work of modern researchers Sh.B.Shaydullaev, A.Sh.Shaydullaev, recalling S.P.Tolstov's opinions about water bodies, concluded that the basis of the farms of the Tozabogyob, Amirabad, and Water bodies of the lower Amu Darya basin in the Bronze Age did not have local roots. who recorded.[69]The authors did not pay attention to the information about the economy in the works of the researchers.

In the second half of the 2nd millennium BC, cattle-breeding tribes that lived in the Southern Urals (Yogochband), Western Kazakhstan (Andronova) were geographically located in the Yonbosh-Kokcha, Anka-Bozarkala and Kavatkala regions, and carried ethnic data.[70] In this historical period, there were changes in quantity and quality of work tools, that is, work tools made of bronze and three-pointed bow arrows were used by the population. The inhabitants of the oasis are engaged in "kayr" farming in the sernam and serunum barrens, and have moved from a self-cultivation farm to a production farm.

---

[69] Матякубов Х. Хоазм воҳаси бронза ва илк темир даври тарихи-Тошкент, 2017, -Б.22

[70] Шайдуллаев Ш.Б, Шайдуллаев А.Ш. "Хоразм" атамасининг пайдо бўлиши ва семантикаси//Хоразм тарихи. Замонавий тадқиқотлар. –Тошкент-Урганч. Наврўз, 2019. – Б. 7

CHAPTER II The kingdom of the ancient state of Khorezm.

The history of our ancestors reflected in legends.

In studying the history of our ancestors who lived in the lower Amu Darya region, along with material objects, folk folklore has gained an important importance. The history of the historical period, the narratives of the villages and cities that allowed the population to develop daily practical economic traditions in its various stages, are preserved in the memory of those who love the history of the land to this day. Construction of some residential areas (Ayozkala-1), Anqakala (legendary bird), Katta Guldursun (treason to the motherland), Qirqqizkala (ayans' resistance to enemies), Almaotishgan (boy and girl throwing apples at each other), Hazorasp (a thousand moons, its arch was built by Suleiman the Giant, legends of a well in the interior of Khiva) have come down to us in publications.

Myths and legends about the ancient cities of Khorezm are the results of folklore. In the legends of the III-IV centuries AD, legends about King Barak are connected with the complex of Baraktom ruins. The king himself lived in the palace in this complex, and his bird of prey, a huge eagle, lived in another palace. The king was cruel and stubborn. One day, his mother, the giant legendary bird Anko, comes to see his eagle. Barak went hunting that day. His friends try to persuade him not to go hunting, telling him not to touch the eagle, but he does not accept the advice of the advisers. Then the insulted eagle took him to the sky with his horse and threw him to the ground. Barak's body is buried in the castle, the region is deserted. From then on, caravans did not enter the cursed place. they bypass. Anqakala is associated with the legend of the Anqo bird. According to legends, once upon a time in Kirqqizkala, there are legends about princess Guloyim Batir, the hero of the Karakalpak epic "Kirqqiz" and her forty friends. Such legendary monuments are located in Central Asia in the Kyrgyz name

Marv, Termiz.[71] The monument of Kirqqiztepa in Khorezm region dates back to the Middle Ages.

An interesting legend about the creation of Ayozkala I is noteworthy. In this legend, one of the rulers of Khorezm announced to the public that he would build a large fortress on its border to protect his country from the attack of an external enemy. For this purpose, he announced that he would give his beautiful daughter in marriage to whoever would build a huge impregnable fortress on the northern border of his country. At that time, there was a shepherd named Ayaz, who began to build the fortress. The king did not keep his word and gave his daughter to someone else. The shepherd Ayoz, who found out about this, stopped the construction, so the castle was left unfinished. In this place, the myth and the truth coincide. In folk legends, this castle is associated with the name of the heroic slave Ayoz, who was a welcomer to the queen who lived in the Kyrgyz castle with his forty friends. In the past, the Aral Sea was inhabited by the Adag people, who were ruled by the cruel and treacherous Fasil Khan. The Baysin people lived in the Uzboy region. This nation was ruled by Ayaz Khan, who was known for his wisdom and justice.

For the terrible crime of Fasil Khan, who insulted the honor of a saint's daughter, the saint prayed for him, and as a result, the whole kingdom of Fasil Khan was submerged. In this place, the Aral Sea appears, and two huge rivers begin to flow into it. After building the confluence of the rivers, the Baysin people moved to Khorezm under the leadership of Ayoz Khan and founded the kingdom called Urgench.[72]Brief information about the existence of the image of Ayaz can be found in Mahmud Koshgari's work "Devonu lug'otit turk" created in the 11th century. It says: "Frost is the name of the slave." The

---

[71] Толстов С.П. По следам древнехорезмийской цивилизации. М.,-Л., АН СССР, 1948, -С. 21-22.
[72] Нестеров А. Прошлое приаральских степей в преданиях киргиз Казалинского уезда. ЗВО. Т. XII. Вмп.ГУ. СПб, 1900, -С, 95-100.

image of Qul Ayaz also appears in the 17th century, in Abulgazi's "Shajarai Tarokima".

Stories about the history of the Big Guldursun monument have been preserved. Until recently, people used to say that this cursed place, that there is an underground passage in the castle guarded by a dragon, and that anyone who tries to search for Guldursun's incalculable wealth will die. There are also various legends about the appearance of the castle. The first information about such legends can be found in the works of A. I. Gerasimovsky. He wrote down the description of the fortress and the legend about the appearance of Guldursun, which he heard from the head of the volost Sadiqboy. The fortress was built by the Iranian king Hasan in connection with the following event. One day, Hasan, who went hunting gazelle with falcons, meets a beautiful Jewish girl. Her name is Zuria, and others call her Malika. Zuria is running away from her father. Hasan took the girl with him and wanted to marry her. However, the girl made a condition that you will build the castle. The king fulfilled her wish and built a fortress, and in the middle of the fortress he erected a pillar dedicated to his young wife. He was named Gul-Sutun (Gulustun). The castle was also called by this name. Over time, this name was corrupted and became Guldursun. Big Guldursun, or rather, Gul-Sutun fortress, was built on a plain. It covers an area of 100 square meters. The castle is surrounded by three rows of walls. There are three constellations on each side: two of them are on either side, and one is in the middle. The fort is built of large-sized bricks. The yard was covered with sand almost to the top of the wall. The fortress is entered from the east, and there is a tower on both sides of the gate.[73] recorded information such as The remains of the defense walls and turrets of Katta Guldursun have been preserved, it is considered one of the objects of cultural heritage.

In the second version of the legend, recorded by Karakalpak scholar U. Kojurov, the name of the fortress is

---

[73] Герасимовский А.И. Древности Хивм и Амударьинского отдела. //Исторический вестник (XVII, сентябрь), 1909, -С, 971-973.

called "Guliston".[74] According to legends, this Tewarak was a prosperous and well-watered city. The city was ruled by an old king who had a beautiful daughter named Guldursun. A calamity will befall this prosperous city - the Kalmyks will invade from the desert, destroying everything on their way. The Kalmyks laid siege to the city, revealing fertile fields and lush gardens. The population defends the city valiantly, the enemy is not strong enough to overcome its resistance. Months pass like this, and then a more terrible evil - hunger - comes to the aid of the invaders. City dwellers are running out of money. People start dying on the streets. The defenders, who were thinned out, were holding weapons in their bare hands. Then the king called the generals and nobles to a consultation.

One of the arrivals offers to try the last resort of survival. It was a very cunning plan. The besieged people of Gulistan bring some of the well-fed bulls to the palace, feed them all the remaining grain in the king's storehouse, and send them out of the city gate.

Not only the besieged, but also the besiegers were suffering from hunger. During the many-month siege, the Kalmyks had eaten everything they could eat, and those in the enemy's camp began to dream of ending the siege. When hungry Kalmaks catch and slaughter bulls, their stomachs are full of grains of wheat. Seeing this, he was confused: "If they feed the cattle with such grain, they have a lot of reserves!" the warriors shout. "The siege is useless, the city cannot be taken, we must leave without dying of hunger." The commanders of the Kalmyks also come to this decision. There is a reluctance to return to the headquarters. But Guldursun, the king's daughter, behaves differently. He was the leader of the Kalmyks from the city wall for many months, young, handsome, brave, A young wrestler was following the Kalmyk prince. His heart was filled with passion for the leader of his people's enemy. A passionate letter from a faithful maid to a Kalmyk knight, who saw that the

---

[74] Толстов С.П. Древний Хорезм. По следам древних культур. М. 1951, 172-173.

cunning of the besiegers had worked, that the enemy's camp was filled with the roar of camels preparing to retreat, that countless Kalmyks were gathered and disappeared from sight, and that within a few hours there would be no trace of them and that she would not be able to see the handsome prince again. writes: "If you wait one more day, you will witness the surrender of the city" and reveals the secret of the besieged. Kalmyks unload their loads from camels, and at night countless bonfires are lit outside the city. In the morning, the people of Gulistan, exhausted from hunger and dying, saw that their tricks did not work and that the enemy surrounded the city even more, surrendered and left themselves to the mercy of the enemy. The city will be looted, set on fire, part of the population will be exterminated, and part will be taken away as slaves. The traitor Guldursun is brought to the presence of the prince. The prince looked at the girl and said: "A girl who betrayed her country, her people and her parents because of her shameless lust for the enemy, what would you do to me if someone set fire to her heart again?" Tie him to the tails of the stallions so that he does not betray anyone else."Guldursun's body, dragged by horses, is scattered all over the field. This place, infected with the cursed blood of the traitor, will be deserted and will be called Guldursun instead of Gulistan. There is a grain of historical truth in this tragic narrative. At the core of the legends of the peoples of Central Asia, under the name of cruel conquerors called Kalmyks, who rode through Kazakhstan and Central Asia in the 17th and 18th centuries with swords and set fire to everything, the more rabid conqueror Genghis Khan's Mongols of the 13th century were hidden. Guldursun fields, which are alive again in our days, died out during the Mongol attack. Popular rumors connect the history of Devkesgan-kala with the legendary Farhad and Shirin, whose love affair is legendary in the East. In the city of Devkesgan, among the ruins of unknown buildings, two nameless mausoleums stand tall. There are two tombs in each of them, and local residents believe that Farhad and Shirin are buried in one of these tombs. According to legend, the mighty Adhamshah ruled the Daryalik and Sarikamish regions in the past. He had a beautiful daughter named Shirin, and in response to the love of stonecutter Farhad, he fell in love with her. Adhamshah, who did not want these two young people to meet at all, and at the same time directly refused and did not want to burn his beloved daughter, announced that he would give his daughter to the person who cut the rocks of Ustyurt, opened a trench and built a fortification. Although Farhad was a master stonemason, he could not do this work alone. However, Shirin is cunning: Farhad digs the mountain during the day, and Shirin forces thousands of her slaves to do this work at night. After some time, they inform Adhamshah that the fort and the moat are ready. The surprised and angry king says that this cannot be done, that there is some difficulty in it, that neither a man nor a giant can build the castle. Nevertheless, it was necessary to keep the promise. The king, who does not want to give sweets to ordinary citizens, also uses a trick: he digs a part of the trench deep for a thousand slaves at night. In the morning, he said to Shirin: "You see, Farhad, whom you love, did not work tonight, the giant did the job. He is a liar, I will not give you to him. Farhad, who could not bear Hijran, dies. The name of the fortress - "Devkesgan" comes from this. Shirin also dies after Farhad. In the southern part of the city, on the edge of the Ustyurt ravine, there are two tombs of these two lovers.[75] Actually Devkesgan or Wazir mil. avv. It has existed since the IV century and its date is determined by the early history of Khorezm, when Amudarya returned to Sarikamishboi. This fortress-city was built on the basis of all the rules of construction of military fortifications used in Khorezm at that time, taking into account the strategic location of the city from the point of view of defense, as well as agricultural problems related to irrigation activities. That is why Devkesgan was built on the remains of a hill in the region on the left bank of the river.

---

[75] Пугаченкова Г.А. Материалы к истории Хорезмского зодчества. //МХЭ. Вьш. 7. М. 1963. –С. 315.

The stories about Farhad, who died trying to cut a rock and open a path to water, and Shirin, who secretly entered this place to sacrifice her life for her lover, are just a beautiful legend full of romantic exaggeration, sincerity and pure emotion. However, this legend attracts many people who come to Devkesgan to circumambulate the land of people they do not know, hoping that fate will give them such a strong and proud feeling that neither time nor migration can extinguish. In the distant past, steeped in legends, the city was destroyed, life in it slowly died out. Only mausoleums are left, which carefully preserve the secrets of the people buried in them. Inside the mausoleums there are spiral staircases, and if you go up to the roof, you can see an endless view of a whirlwind that rarely rises before your eyes. It is believed that the legend of Devkesgan originated in the 7th century, before the conquest of Iran by the Arabs, based on the love of the Iranian king Khusraw II Parviz (590-628) for Princess Shirin, recorded in the Sassanid palace annals. This legend was also included in Firdawsi's Shahnama. There are various legends about the names of these heroes among the people. In Nizami's epic "Khusrav and Shirin", the image of Farhad, an ordinary craftsman and stonecutter, who fell in love with the beautiful Shirin, appears. This hero's love remains unrequited. The historical and geographical reality of these eastern epics is connected with a rather large area of Central Asia and partially the Caucasus. Therefore, it is impossible to determine exactly where the events took place. The popularization of the legend about Farhad and Shirin naturally expands the range of real historical places where the events described in it may have happened. It seems that this legend has a mythological basis. An ancient underworld god,[76]

At the beginning of the 20th century, Sultan Uwais went to the Govur fortress on the mountain A.E. Rossikova tells the following legend about the castle. Once upon a time, there lived

---

[76] Толстов С.П. По следам древнехорезмийской цивилизации. М.,-Л., АН СССР, 1948, -С. 24.

a pious man named Shish Prophet in the city of Kipchak. He had a beautiful wife, and a young, handsome rich man named Govur fell in love with her. The woman is also interested in him, but Visol has no choice. Govur decided to build a fort on a nearby mountain and build an underground path (lahm) from it to his mistress. The castle and the castle were finished, and the lovers began to go to each other's houses. Visol days continued more or less. One day, the woman's husband came out on top of them. In a fit of rage, he threw himself at Govur, trying to kill him. No matter how young and strong Govor is, he cannot defeat a pious husband. A tired lover looks at his lover pleadingly, as if asking for help. The mistress understands the meaning of this look, takes a handful of millet and scatters it under her husband's feet. Then her husband's foot slips and he squats down, but he is not confused. Convinced that his wife is helping his lover, a pious man calls his beloved dog to help. The dog pounces on Govur and bites his leg. Moisafid kills the fallen Govur, then looks at his unfaithful wife and says: "He learned to help his master from a dog." However, his wife does not show any remorse and goes into her room. Unable to bear his anger, Shish killed the prophet's wife. Before his death, he bequeathed to his children only to bury his body, and to cut off his legs and throw them away. After death, the children do as their father told them: they bury the body,

A.E. Rossikova wrote, half of the Govur fortress was destroyed, the buildings were also damaged by time, but in general, these ruins give the impression of a terrible fortress in which several dozen people have taken refuge. It seems that the fortress was abandoned by the people after Tsarist Russia conquered Khiva and lost its strategic importance, writes the researcher.[77] According to the legend of Chilpiq recorded by A. Vamberi, this castle was the place of a princess who fell in love with her father's slave and could not get parental consent and lived with her lover. A.E. Rossikova cites a legend about the

---

[77] Россикова А.Е. По Амударье от Петро-Александровска до Нукуса. Русский Вестник, август, 1902, -С. 641-643.

construction of Chilpiq, which she heard from local residents: "Chilpiq kala was built by an eunuch named Chilpiq. During the construction of the fortress wall, mud fell from his hands, and the high tower, whose ruins are still preserved on the hillside, was created from this mud. Its flat top, which remains within the fortress walls, is rocky. All the rocks are full of Arabic writing, some hieroglyphs and incomprehensible drawings.

Ethnographer G.P.Snesarev, an employee of the Khorezm archaeological expedition, recorded another legend about the Chilpik kala. Here is the legend: "Dev Haji Muluk built the Chilpiq kala on the right bank of the Amu Darya. The giant was carrying clay with his huge hands to build a wall: then a lump of clay fell from between his fingers and now lies next to him as the foundation of the wall. In Chilpiq, they still show the hill on the ground where Haji Muluk "lived". There is another legend about Chilpiq, according to which the fortress was built by another giant - Karatin Alp. Among local residents, there is another legend related to the functional name of Chilpiq. This legend essentially reveals the main function of the monument as a Zoroastrian shrine.

According to the legend, "in ancient times, old people were taken out on a mountain or a high hill. One day, a young man decided to take his old father up a high mountain. The boy's name is Chilpiq. He is climbing the mountainside and sits down on the middle rock to rest. Then his father laughed. The young man asked why you are laughing, I will leave you on the hill. His father, I was also taking my father out of this way, sitting on this stone and resting. He said that he laughed when he remembered that incident. The young man took his father back and took care of him secretly. According to the custom of that time, the young man could be sentenced to death for this act. After some time, the king of this country fell ill. None of the doctors brought from all over the country could cure him. Then the young man's father told him the name of a herb and advised him that if he drinks its tincture, the king will find a cure. The young man went and told the king the name of the herb and told him that he would be cured if he drank its tincture. The king who drank the infusion was indeed cured. Then the king asked the young man, "The doctors called from all over the country could not cure me. How did you know this tincture?" The young man said that if you pass a spoonful of my blood, I will reveal the secret. After the king forgave his sin, the young man told everyone that he had been taking care of his father secretly. Hearing this incident, the king issued a decree not to take the old people out of the mountain and to take care of them until the end of their lives. This myth, apparently,

According to the legend spread among the inhabitants of the town of Beruni, who lived around it, Pilkala was built by the ruler of Khorezm to keep the elephants that he presented to the Sultan of Hind, Khorezmshah. The name of the castle comes from this. The castle is square in shape, surrounded by a defensive wall on both sides.

The founding of the Kokhnauaz fortress, located 40 km west of Tashkhovuz (Turkmenistan), is associated with the name of the legendary Sa'di Waqqas, who lived during the reign of the fourth caliph Ali. It is also possible that Sa'di Waqqas is a changed form of the name Sa'd ibn Abi Waqqas, who was one of the companions of Prophet Muhammad.

Stories related to the history of Khorezm and its cities were known even in the Middle Ages. Muqaddasiy cites the following legend in his work "Ahsan al-taqasim fi ma'rifat al-aqalim" ("The best classifications for learning about climates"): according to the narration, in ancient times, the ruler of the East angered 400 people from the inhabitants of his country and took them 100 farsakhs away from the place where people live. ordered to leave. That place is now Kas (city). After some time, he sent his men to get news from them. When they went and looked, they found that people were alive, they had built their houses, and they were making a living by catching fish. There is also a lot of firewood. They returned and informed the king about it. "What do they call meat?" - asked the king. "Khor" (or "khvar"), they answered. "What about the wood?" "Razm", -

was the answer. Then the king said: "I gave that land to them and called this place Khorazm." He ordered to take 400 Turkish girls there. That's why they still look like Turks. In Yakut (XIII century) we find the following interesting information about Kat: Kat is the ancient capital of Khorezm. It is located on the eastern bank of Jayhun, opposite Jurjania. After it was flooded, its inhabitants moved to the place where they live now. It is narrated that the Messenger of Allah Muhammad saw this city during his journey to a distant mosque at night. It is narrated that in the twelfth year of Prophethood, in the month of Rabi ul-Awwal, they went from the synagogue in Makkah to Quddus Sharif at night. from there they ascended to the throne. It is called the "Night of Miraj" and it is also mentioned in the Qur'anic Majid (XVII).[78]

---

[78] Ғ.Ходжаниязов. Қадимги Хоразм мудофаа иншоотлари. Тошкент, "O'ZBEKISTON", 2007. –С, 22.

2.2 Secrets of Aqchakhankala and Tuproqkala.

Information about the history of Khorezm's independence from the Achaemenid dynasty is recorded differently in the works of researchers. For example, Aqchakhanqala, registered by the Khorezm expedition stafflt is located in Beruni district. S.P.Tolstov said that the monument belongs to the Kushon-African period.[79] In 1982-1985, as a result of the excavations carried out by G. Khojaniyazov at the monument, the date of the fortress area and the system of its defense walls was re-analyzed. Since 1995, the staff of the archaeological team, established in cooperation with the Karakalpakstan branch and the University of Sydney, Australia, started digging at the monument.[80] It has been determined that there are three construction periods in the monument. During the first construction period, a two-row straw wall was built, its height is 1-1.30 m, width is 2.50 m. The wall of the one cubit labyrinth in front of the gate was also restored from thatch (size 60x120 m). During the second construction period, a thatched wall and a square brick wall (40x40x10cm) were built on the tower walls. The change in the size of the corridor is not noticeable. In front of the gate is a complex structure with a wall made of square bricks. During the third construction period, due to the construction of the square brick wall, its height is 7 m, and its thickness is 5 m. The gate labyrinth wall has no constellations. The monument has a square shape, it consists of an inner and an outer part. The total volume is 55 ha. The area of the inner castle is 13 hectares, and it is surrounded by a two-line wall with a

---

[79] Андрианов. Б. В. Дрение оросительные системы Приаралья. М. «Наука», 1969, с. 135.

[80] Хожаниёзев. Г. Оқшахон ёки тарихда минг йил жумбоқ бўлиб келган номаълум қалъа ҳақида//Жайхун, №1//.Нукус., 1998. Хожаниёзев. Г. Х., Ягодин. В.Н., Хелмс. С.У., Макларен. Б.К. Раскопки на Ақшаханкалы//Археологические исследования в Узбекистане в 2001г//. Самарканд, 2000., Хожаниёзев. Г. Х., Хелмс. С.У., Снеддон. Э. Археологические исследования на городе Ақшаханкала в 2001 году//Археологические исследования в Узбекистане в 2001г//. Самарканд, 2002, с. 165-167. Ягодин. В. Н., Ходжаниязов. Г. Х., Статов. В. А. Внешняя стена городища Казаклы-Яткан// Ўзбекистон тарихи моддий ва ёзма манбаларда//. Т., "Фан", 2005, с. 172-178.

corridor 2.32 m wide. The thickness of the outer wall is 1.70 m, and the inner wall is 2 m. The corner of the wall is square, and the area between them is 27 m. On the outer wall and rectangular towers there are spear-pointed tires with an interval of 1.3-1.4 m. An additional wall was built on the outer wall, its thickness is 3.60-4.60. The additional wall is made of square bricks (41x43x41x43x11.14cm). The lower part is also surrounded by a square wall with two rows, its width is 1.23-1.43 cm. height 0.-1.55 m. Ark-Alo is located in the northwest corner of the city, its area is 1.3 hectares. An additional wall was built to the wall of the arch, traces of a trench were preserved near it. The thickness of the outer wall is 2.8-3 m, and the inner part is 1.9-2 m, the width of the corridor is 2.5-3 m. The wall, in turn, has rectangular towers with a size of 9 m. The upper city has four gates. The peshdarvozas are fortified with a false road and an additional wall, and they do not have a tower.[81] It has been determined that Akshakhanqala ceramics consists of three chronological periods: the Late Archaic, Kanguy and Kushon periods. Ceramics of the first group. avv. He came to the conclusion that he or V-IV centuries, the second - IV-III centuries BC-I centuries AD, and the ceramics of the third group corresponded to II-V centuries.[82] The remains of the stelobad preserved at a certain height were demolished, assuming it to be the ruler's tomb. This building is academician According to A. Askarov's conclusion, the main bonfire was the fire that was visible from afar. The area of its lowest preserved part, the platform, is 60 m. According to the logical conclusion, the highest circle was reduced to 4x4 meters, and the main altar was placed on it. This pyre was a structure dedicated to the sun god, where an eternal fire burned. There are 12 constellations on the outer northern wall of the capital, 7 in the east, 4 in the west,

---

[81] Хожаниёзов. F.Х. Хоразм мудофаа иншоотлари. Т, "Ўзбекистон", 2007, 6. 32-34.

[82] Ходжаниязов. Г. К. Фортификация древнего Хорезма(VI в. до н.э. - IVв.н.э. У/АКД//. Нукус., 1996, с. 6. Ходжаниязов. Г. К., Хелмс. С. У., Снеддон. Э. Археологические исследования на городе Ақшаханка 2001 году//Археологические исследования в Узбекистане в 2001г// Самарканд, 2002, с. 170.

and 5 in the south. The remains of 28 square and rectangular towers have been preserved in the defense walls of Akshakhan. The city was the political center of Khorezm in the IV-III centuries BC.

Tuproqkala (Ellikkala). The general plan of the fortress was developed by the Khorezm expedition. In 1945-1950, when the Khorezm expedition carried out excavations in Tuproqkala Palace, new rare and invaluable resources were obtained.[83]In 1967-1976, Y.E.Nerazik and Y. A. Rapoport continued archaeological work in Tuproqkala.[84]

In the 80s of the 20th century, researchers continued the excavation work in Tuproqkala, and a monograph was published on the items found.[85]With this, the second monograph, summarizing the results of the research conducted in the palace part, was brought to the attention of the scientific community.[86]More than 30 houses and rooms have been opened and studied in Tuproqkala palace. The monument is located in Ellikkala District. From the place where Tozabogyob and Kirqqizkala separated, the Tuproqkala irrigation facility was built to the northwest, and Tuproqkala was built on the plain. It has a rectangular shape in the plane, and its size (500x340 m), i.e. 17 ha. It has been determined that the construction of the city consists of three historical periods. In the period of the first historical date, it was surrounded by two rows of thatched walls, between which the corridor was 3 m wide. The thickness of the outer wall is 2.20 m, and the inner part is 1.20 m. The total wall

---

[83] Толстов С.П. По древним дельтам Окса и Яксарта. М. "Наука", 1962, с. 204-226

[84] Неразик. Е. Е. Раскопки городища Топраккала/КСИА АН СССР//, №132, М.,1972, с. 23.43.Ўша муаллиф. Раскопки городища Топраккала// АО 1974.-М. »Наука» 1975.-С.508-509., Рапопорт Ю.А., Гертман А.Н. Работы на Топраккале //АО 1976//. М., «Наука» 1977, с 539-540.

[85] Городище Топрак-кала(Раскопки 1965-1975г)//ТХЛЭЭ//. Т. Х11, М., Наука» 1981.

[86] Топрак-калъа (Дворец)//ГХАЭЭ//. Т. XIV, М. »Наука», 1984.

thickness is 6.40 m. The outer wall extends from the side to a distance of 5.50-6 m, and the space between them is 27 m.

In the center of the southern wall of the monument there is a gate, which in turn is protected by a one-cubic rectangular thatched building (size 55x65 m). During the second construction period, the outer and inner thatched walls are lined with square brick walls (40x40x10 cm). The wall in front of the gate will be rebuilt from square bricks, and as a result, it will also be adjusted upwards. In the northwestern corner of the city there is an arch (size 180x180 m), the square constellations in its corners are preserved 14 m. In this historical period, the walls of the square brick defensive wall, the tower and the front of the gate were studded with spears, they were located at a distance of 1.10-1.30 cm from each other, their inner part was 20 cm wide, and the inner part was 0.60 cm high. , 1.70 m long lancet tires on the outer side with the exit directed downwards. During the third construction period, rectangular corridors with a rounded shape were built on the upper part of the brick wall, the remains of which have been preserved in the walls of the northern and northeastern corners. There are 4 rectangular towers on the outer north wall, 12 on the east, 12 on the west, and 4 on the south (total number of rectangular and square towers is 32). In front of the outer gate, the labyrinthine wall, which forms a defensive area, is free of towers. In general, the outer defensive wall of Tuproqkala had 32 square and rectangular towers. The outer and inner walls were connected by an archway wall, the width of the corridor between them was 2.50 cm. It was the summer residence of the African state. Cultural life continued in the arch part of the city until the 7th century AD.

CHAPTER III Religious beliefs of Khorezm residents.

3.1 Religious beliefs of the settled population and Zoroastrianism.

It is located like an island between Kyzylkum and Karakum. For the history of the spiritual culture of our ancestors, who lived in the Khorezm oasis from the earliest times, periodization based on the summary of the existence of written sources and the achievements of archeology. learning with is important. S.P.Tolstov, a researcher of the history of Khorezm, who brought the huge achievements in the material and spiritual culture of the people who lived in this legendary land into the science of world history, in his first work, the archaeological culture of the achievements of our ancestors in the spiritual sphere during the period of history that lasted until the early Middle Ages. on the basis of:

- Hunters and Gatherers of Caltaminor Culture (Yonbosh-4).
- Suvyorgan and Tozabogyob culture.
- Amirabad culture (early iron age of VIII-VII centuries BC).
- Archaic period culture - BC. VI-V centuries.
- Kangli-Kanha culture - BC. IV-I century AD.
- Kushan culture - II-V centuries AD.
- Culture of the African period - VI-IX centuries.

The periodization of the historical process of the researcher from the analysis of new archeological objects taken from the settlements of the population was published, which noted some changes in the spiritual culture. The fact that the Kang' culture is not related to Khorezm (it is related to the middle basin of Syrdarya), the Kushan period is not related to Khorezm. The history of the legendary land is ancientized by the activities of hunters of the Late Stone, Mesolithic and Early Neolithic periods. In the foothills of Sultan Uwais, hunters of the Late Stone, Mesolithic, and Early Neolithic periods attributed their religious beliefs to miracles occurring in nature during their daily activities. That is, from the time they came into the world of literature and the world, they were left in the vortex of various phenomena that occur in nature, and they were powerless in front of the works of nature. The source of knowledge of the human being born in this world is related to his daily work. It is known that the knowledge and practical experience he gathered in the process of work was created under the influence of natural phenomena. It should be noted that man is influenced by the environment around him, i.e. the natural environment, flora and fauna, natural phenomena, and the beliefs and trusts of man in them. S.P.Tolstov was able to describe the beliefs of hunters and gatherers who found a place in the Neolithic site of Jonbos-4, that is, in the archeologically studied circular shape (1.2 m in circumference) in the middle of the interior of the cave. noted that the fireplace "gave constant heat". The campfire was sacred for the clan community of 100-120 people. It is known that the knowledge and practical experience he gathered in the process of work was created under the influence of natural phenomena. It should be noted that man is influenced by the environment around him, i.e. the natural environment, flora and fauna, natural phenomena, and the beliefs and trusts of man in them. S.P.Tolstov was able to describe the beliefs of hunters and gatherers who found a place in the Neolithic site of Jonbos-4, that is, in the archeologically studied circular shape (1.2 m in circumference) in the middle of the interior of the cave. noted that the fireplace "gave constant heat". The campfire was sacred for the clan community of 100-120 people. It is known that the knowledge and practical experience he gathered in the process of work was created under the influence of natural phenomena. It should be noted that man is influenced by the environment around him, i.e. the natural environment, flora and fauna, natural phenomena, and the beliefs and trusts of man in them. S.P.Tolstov was able to describe the beliefs of hunters and gatherers who found a place in the Neolithic site of Jonbos-4, that is, in the archeologically studied circular shape (1.2 m in circumference) in the middle of the interior of the cave. noted that the fireplace "gave constant heat". The campfire was sacred for the clan community of 100-

120 people. natural phenomena are created by people's beliefs and trust in them. S.P.Tolstov was able to describe the beliefs of hunters and gatherers who found a place in the Neolithic site of Jonbos-4, that is, in the archeologically studied circular shape (1.2 m in circumference) in the middle of the interior of the cave. noted that the fireplace "gave constant heat". The campfire was sacred for the clan community of 100-120 people. natural phenomena are created by people's beliefs and trust in them. S.P.Tolstov was able to describe the beliefs of hunters and gatherers who found a place in the Neolithic site of Jonbos-4, that is, in the archeologically studied circular shape (1.2 m in circumference) in the middle of the interior of the cave. noted that the fireplace "gave constant heat". The campfire was sacred for the clan community of 100-120 people.[87]During this period, the Neolithic clan communities living in the foothills of South Turkmenistan, which is a hot region of Central Asia, and in the vicinity of the Murgob river, have been archaeologically studied, as well as special religious buildings and house temples with small sculptures. In the south, the spiritual culture of the sedentary agricultural population, accustomed to the conditions of the Karakum desert, was manifested by ceramic figurines of people and domestic animals, birds and animals decorated with ornaments, amulets, and pottery.[88]So, it is possible to imagine the religious-ideological views of the sedentary agricultural population of the Neolithic period through material objects. But such beliefs were not found in clan communities in the Khorezm oasis, not only from the Neolithic, but also from the Eneolithic (middle of the 4th millennium BC - the first half of the 3rd millennium BC) period. In the spirituality of our ancestors, there was a desire for fire, which determined the content of social life.

However, when it came to the Bronze Age (the second half of the 3rd millennium BC - the 2nd millennium BC),

---

[87] Толстов С.П. Қадимги Хоразм маданиятини излаб. – Тошкент, Фан, 1964 – Б. 78

[88] Сарианиди В.Ы. Культовые здания поселений анауской культуры//СА – М, 1962 №1-С. 44-47, Хлопик И.Ж. Геоисторская группа поселений эпохо энеолита.- М-Л.: Наука, 1964.-С.76-79.

fundamental changes took place in the spirituality of our ancestors. According to M.A. Itina, horse and dog and female figurines made of clay and dried in the sun were taken from the settlements belonging to the Tozabogyob culture.[89]In the monographs of scientists on the history of the culture of the Bronze Age, the existence of livestock farming and the customs of their worship were recorded in the clay statues.[90]In fact, these material objects indicate that the beliefs of totemism and fertility were established in the spirituality of the population living in the area of the Lower Amudarya basin. The study of horses and sheep indicates that our ancestors not only practiced fine arts and the process of formation in their daily activities, but also the development of horses and the care of domestic animals with light hooves. Of course, the views and beliefs of our ancestors in the Neolithic, Eneolithic and Bronze Age (fire worship, totemism, fertility) were created under the influence of socio-economic scientists. Their formation continued in later historical periods. According to research, BC. Until the 7th century, the population settled in the lower Amu Darya basin developed a culture of urban planning (dwellings were in the form of basements).[91]In S.P.Tolstov's researches, some of the outdated ideas about the historical period inhabited by Khorezm oasis residents, the economic and ethno-cultural relations they carried out in their daily activities in the last stages were preserved. As an example, A.A.Skorov pointed out that these views are outdated and that they should be reconsidered.[92] This issue is further addressed in subsequent publications.[93] In the course of

---

[89] Итина М.А. Женская статуэтка элоль ранней бронза из Хорезм//КСИЭ- М: 1958, Вып XXX – С.23-29.

[90] Итина М.А. История етелиных премен южного Приоралья (II – югило I тысяче летие до ы-7)//ТрХАЭЭ,-М,: 1977, Т-С. 138. Рис-69

[91] Сагдуллаев А.С, Матякубов Х.К Проблеме происхождение глинобытно сырцовой архитектуры в Хоразме/Вестник Национарьнаго Университета Узбекистана. – Ташкент:,2013. Спец выпуск – С.59-64.

[92] Аскаров А Қадимги Хоразм тарихига оид баъзи бир масалалар//Ўзбекистон этнологияси: Янгича карашлар ва ёндашувлар – Тошкент, 2004. Б 76-84

[93] История государственности Узбекистана. – Ташкент, «Узбекистан» - Т-1. –С. 106-126.: Хорезм в истории государственносто Узбекистана – Ташкент.: «Узбекистан», 2013-С. 14-29.

our ancestors living in an ancient society and conducting economic activities, small and large horned cattle and horse statues were taken from the houses of the Yakkaporsan-2 settlement, which was built in the form of a semi-basement.[94]

So, the Yakkaporsons, the descendants of the Tozabogyobs, who farmed in the area of the Southern Aralboi basin in the IX-VIII centuries BC, along with the culture of artificial irrigation farming, took care of light and heavy ungulates in domestic livestock. traditions, sanctifying them, reflected them in the statues.

In the 7th-6th centuries BC, the history of Khorezm's population underwent unique ethnic-cultural considerations. In particular, such relations developed in the southwest of the Khorezm oasis, in the southwest of the Amudarya Davdan tributary, around the Kuyisoi heights. The people who settled in the height of Kuyisoi are known as Sakas in historical literature.[95]In fact, the people of Yakkaporson settled in the vicinity of Kuyisoy Heights at the beginning of the 7th century BC. How did they become sacks?

The burial structures of the Kuysoys have been archaeologically studied, apparently those who have passed awayperformed in cremation belief.

The inhabitants of yakkaparsanian abandoned their familiar geographical area forever, developed animal husbandry from the lush flora of the Kuyisoi Heights, and carried out their faith by practicing "nomadic agriculture".

In the publications of the researchers, the changes that occurred in the spirituality of the inhabitants of the early Iron Age in Khorezm were brought to the region from the lands of the lower Syr Darya.It is connected with the migration of a

---

[94] Итина М.А История степных племен........-С.210.

[95] Вайнберг Б.И. Паметника Кս۸юсайекой культуры/Кочевники на границах Хорезме. ТрХАЭЭ – М,: 1979. Т-XI-С. 45-52. Ўша муаллиф. Скобоворческие племени в древнем Хорезма – М.Наука, 1981-С.121-124.

group of representatives of the people who migrated, Murgob and Bactria.[96]In the 7th-6th centuries BC, the inhabitants of the lower Amu Darya basin lived surrounded by the world of nomads and conducted practical training on ethnic relations in the geography of the designated area. Nomadic herders settled on the eastern side of the Khorezm oasis, that is, around the Syr Darya Ingordarya tributary, were neighbors with Kuyisoy herders in the southwest (Sariqamishboi basin). At this historical date, in the north-eastern area of the Sarikamishboi basin, in the highlands where the middle part of the Amudarya is connected to the foot of the left bank, the people who showed ethnic relations lived in the Kuzalikir kala. They made good use of straw and raw bricks and carried out farming culture. The castle is surrounded by a two-line defensive wall on different sides. The structure of the interior of the monument is a palace,[97]

But there is no information about the constructions of the Kuzalqir kala. According to the work of the Greek historian Herodotus, in the last quarter of the 6th century BC, Khorezm was included in the Achaemenid state, and together with Parthia, Areia, and Sugd, it formed the 16th satrapy.[98] In this period, the inhabitants of the oasis kept the cremation of the dead. Because burial structures are not recorded in archaeological sources. However, starting from the 5th century BC, a fundamental change in religious beliefs took place in the spirituality of the population. Clay ossuaries (circular-domed, square) were found in one of the Kalaliqir houses belonging to these historical periods, in which the bones of the deceased were found.[99]

---

[96] Сагдуллаев А.С, Матякубов Х.К Проблеме происхождения…. –С 61-63.

[97] Вишневская О.А, Рапопорт Ю.А. Городшие Кюзели-гыр. К вопросу о раннеи этапы истории Хорезма//ВДИ – М,:1997,№2.С 150-155

[98] Герадот. История. В десяти книгх/ Пер Г.А.Стратановского: - Л-Д,: Наука 1972-Кн III. 93.

[99] Рапопорт Ю.А Хорезмийские астодоны//С7,-М.:1962, №4-С. 79.

During the period of influence of the political and economic characteristics of Achaemenids in the main agricultural oases of Uzbekistan, the process of development of various branches of crafts on the basis of settled life was accelerated. Such radical changes in terms of quantity and quality also began in the Khorezm oasis. The viceroy appointed to manage Khorezm by the Achaemenids took Kalaliqir as the capital and started a policy of appropriating the right and left territories. For this purpose, at the beginning of the 5th century BC, in connection with the construction of an irrigation system from the Amudarya towards Kyzylkum, Bozorkala and Dingilja farming micro-oases were created in the plains connected to its coastal foothills.[100]

However, there are no comments regarding the archeological study of the graves that housed the deceased from these population centers. In Kharhol, there is a state of cremation of the dead in the spirituality of the people (in the people of the right bank), and it is possible that their ashes were thrown into the Kalta Minar irrigation facility. In these historical and cultural objects, there is no information about the remains of temples built from clay. Fireplaces are located in the houses. This sacred fireplace is located in Dingilja house.[101]Khumbuztepa, located in the south of Khorezm at the height of the Amu Darya River at Toshsoka, was also studied in such fire pits.[102]From the end of the 5th century BC, after the people of Khorezm became independent from the political and economic influence of the Achaemenids, in the spiritual life of our ancestors, following the wisdom recorded in the book of Avesta, mentioned by Zoroaster, the purity of nature, keeping the soil clean, farming and animal husbandry who carried out

---

[100] Толстов С.П. Древности верхнего Хорезма//ВДИ –М,:1941№2-С.178. Ўша муаллиф Городища с итилыми стенами// КСИИМК-М,:1947.ВЫП XVII-С.3-8 Ўша муаллиф. Древний Хорезм-М,:МГУ.1948-С. 79-80.

[101] Воробъева М.Г. Дингилъдже. Чадьба середины I тысячелетия до.н.7.в Древнем Хорезме//МХЭ, М,:1973, Вып-9.-С.16-17.

[102] Болелов С.Б Некоторые итор археологи чесних работ на Хумбузтепе// Ону, - Ташкент. 1999, -10. –С. 25-90

the policy of development of their villages in an intensive manner. BC Farozman, the founder of the Siyovush-Kayani dynasty, who ruled the Khorezm state until the beginning of the IV-III centuries, Kaykhusrav and his descendants built small and medium-sized settlements in the right and left regions of the Amudarya in a comprehensive manner, in which the fire station - It is known from the works of the Khorezm expedition that the temples were active. The inhabitants of the oasis believed in the power of the forces of nature until the time of Zarathustra. those who expected salvation from them: the belief of burying the dead prevailed. In the south of Khorezm, in the house of Kalaliqir belonging to the 5th century BC, the bones of the dead were dried in ossuaries (masters) made of clay, stone and wood of various shapes. In this way, the people who lived in the north of the Davdon tributary of the Amu Darya basin of the Sarikamishboi basin started their activities for the first time for the purity of the soil by living in irrigated agriculture, livestock raising, and living in thatched and rectangular dwellings. However, in order to keep the soil clean, the settled people who did economic work in the areas of the Lower Amu Darya basin may have mixed the deceased with the water at the place where the irrigation system was released from the Amu Darya. It is believed that a well-irrigated area will increase the amount of productivity. was. Information about the religious beliefs of the inhabitants of the Khorezm oasis is clearly evidenced in the book of Avesta. In particular, the belief of the people of Central Asia in natural phenomena is given a wide place in written sources. In this regard, it is considered to shed light on the religious beliefs of our ancestors regarding natural phenomena. In fact, the book of Avesta contains a lot of cult myths related to the mysteries of nature.

Cult of the sun - it is known that since the human being stepped into this world, he remained in the vortex of natural phenomena. One such phenomenon is the sun. According to the researcher, the sun, its light, in turn, gave rise to the cult of lighting.[103]

According to the work of J. Frazer, the worship of the sun made the sun holy by considering fire as the basis of social life.[104]About the cult, I. Jumanazarov said, "A nation that has a strong belief in fire worships the sun," and T.Jovliyev said, "The fact that people light a fire and jump over it means that they worship the sun." explained their opinions.[105] Nowadays, when a representative of the population goes out of the house, he pays attention to the blue sky, i.e. the sun has risen, and believes that it will be hot today. According to the Avesta scholar M. Isakov, the Uzbek scientist, "The sun is defined as the main source of existence" and it is called "Khurshed Yasht" in the Avesta book dedicated to the glory of the sun.[106]

According to the scientist, the sun is depicted as flying horses and is the source of life that radiates its light, and worshiping its temperature is interpreted as giving life, i.e.

Who are the three horses?

We worship it.

He is a sun-unquenchable flame.

We strive for it.[107]

So, worshiping the sun and enjoying its heat served as the basis for the results achieved by man in his daily activities.

---

[103] Афанасьев. А.Н Поэтические возрения славян на природы – М,:1965.Т.1.-С.117.

[104] Фрезер Дж Золотие веть – М,: Полиёиздей 1990.-С.712.

[105] Жуманазаров У. Тарих, афсона ва дин – Тошкент,: Ўзбекистон, 1990-Б.34. Жавлиев Т. Табиат, инсон ва дин. – Тошкент, Фан, 1986 – Б.21-22.

[106] Искоков М. Авесто. Хуршед Яшт//Ўзбек тили ва адабиёти.-Ташкент,: 1999. №5.Б.72.

[107] Авесто. Яшт китоби/М.Исхоков таржимаси. – Тошкент: "Шарқ" 2001:Б.36.

Cult of the stars - the inhabitants of the Khorezm oasis had an important role in observing the temperature of the stars and appointing a representative to carry out daily practical information on this basis.

Uzbek folklorist scientist M. Jorayev said about the mystery of the stars: "The belief of the seven pirates who became stars dates back to the Altai period in the history of the Turkish population. "The image of the seven robber patrons is one of the most ancient beliefs in folk art."[108]

There are many Uzbek women with the name Yulduz in our daily life. For example, Yulduz, Yulduzkhan, Zuhra, Qambar, etc., each has its own star.

In the "Mehr Yasht" part of the Avesta, the following is noted about the sun of Mithras:

We worship Mithras...

He is the greatest god.

The Holy Spirit is at dawn

The creator is capable of it.

This is the one who created it.

Bright when the moon is full

Bright face with light

Supposedly, Saturn is a star.[109]

Fire cult - one of the most sacred symbols in Zoroastrianism is fire. In Khorezm region, Neolithic (IV-III millennia) clan communities worshiped fire for the first time. For example, in S.P. Tolstov's scientific and popular work, the

---

[108] Жўраев М Ўзбек халқ эътиқодларида сирли рақамлар – Тошкент: Фан, 1991 – Б. 119-120

[109] Авесто. Яшт китоби/М.Исохоқов таржимаси – Тошкент, "Шарқ", 2001. – Б.15.

belief of the hunter-gatherers who made the location Yonbosh-4 was fire.[110] In the ancient Avestan Book of Yasht, the cult of Fire is given a large place.

Water cult - In the cultural and economic regions of Central Asia, the belief in water was important in the population engaged in irrigated agriculture. In Zoroastrianism, water was a sacred drink. There is water - there is life, the waterless area has turned into a desert, such a geographical landscape is depicted before the eyes of a traveler.

In "Khurshed Yasht" of Avesta, it found its meaning in legends about the sanctity of flowing waters and stagnant waters that reflected the sunlight, i.e.

when the sun rises high

The land given by Mazda is bright.

Flowing water glistens,

Hot spring waters.

All species are alive.

Holy Spirits.

At sunrise

The land given by Mazda is hot

Running waters are sacred

Springs are also meritorious.[111]

In verse 25 of the part of the Avesta called "Seven springs of Yasht", the relationship to water is as follows: Finally, we praise

---

[110] Толстов С.П. Қадимги Хоразм маданиятини излаб – Тошкент,:Фан, 1965. – Б.77-78.

[111] Авесто. Яшт китоби//И.Исохоқов таржимаси.-Тошкент, "Шарқ", 2001-Б 36.

the waters, O waters! You are fluent in goodness. We honor the earth.[112]

Announcement   In the published publications, the inhabitants of the Lower Amudarya region believed in the sun, water, moon and animals and sanctified them.[113]

Beliefs about the properties of water are occasionally used in modern vernacular languages. For example, in Gurlan district, women who were drawing water from the well during the day were told that the women passengers would not draw water until they passed.[114]

According to Zoroastrian philosophy, water taken from a well or a ditch early in the morning, when the sun had just risen above the horizon and cast its golden rays over the land, was considered blessed and holy. In the course of field research, it was witnessed that in some areas of Gurlan district of Khorezm region, water is still taken from wells on the bank of the stream after sunrise. After dark, nobody gets water from the well.[115]

According to informants, the lid of the well is closed as soon as it gets dark, because there is a magical belief that in the dark, various demons and wrinkles fall into the water and pollute it.

In the village of Sarapoyon, water is safe. Those who temporarily leave home for a certain period of time for work, study and other purposes are sprinkled with water. It means going as fast as water and returning as fast as water.[116]

---

[112] Авесто. Тарихий-адабий ёдгорлик. А. Маҳкамов таржимаси – Тошкет, Шарқ, 2001.Б 227.

[113] Матякубов Х. Хоразм воҳаси бронза асри ва илк темир даври тарихи// Алишер номидаги Ўзбекистон миллий кутибхонаси нашриёти – Тошкент 2017. – Б. 144-154.

[114] Informant, prof., assoc. Q. Sobirov

[115] Field notes. Umid Bekmukhammed, Gurlan city, Khorezm region, 2013.

[116] Information on the population of the village of Sarapoyon

The views of the population as a precipitant of water. There are also sayings such as not to go near a large canal or ditch, that there are demons and wrinkles in it, and you don't know how you fell into the water, and the intended purpose is to keep children alone aimed at preventing bathing in water bodies.[117]

Also, in the explanatory dictionary of the Uzbek language, you can find the expression "Tagiga suv quydi". The meaning of this is used in the sense of putting someone's work to the test. This is also a phrase directly related to the nature of water. There are many popular water expressions like this. The reason for this is that the daily economic activities of the population are directly related to water. After all, our people have been engaged in agriculture based on artificial irrigation since time immemorial

---

[117]My records of the village of Sarapoyon

3.2 Religious-ideological centers.

Khorezm separated from the Achaemenid state as an independent state, and the researchers of the history of the Khorezm state under the leadership of Farazman do not have a new idea. According to the information provided by the researchers, Khorezm population became independent from Achaemenid influence in the IV century BC.[118]

M.A. Dandamayev said that Khorezm people fulfilled their tax obligations during the period of Artaxerxes II (404-359 BC).[119] B.Y.Stavisky, Khorezm was part of the Achaemenid Empire in the 5th-4th centuries, or in the first half of the 4th century.[120] People of Khorezm, researcher of the ancient world U.R.Rapoport defined the last stage of the Achaemenid rule as the end of the 5th century BC - the first half of the 4th century BC.[121] According to V. I. Weinberg's research, the independence of Khorezm dates back to 1000 BC. It is recorded that it was in the middle of the 4th century.[122] According to A.S.Balakhvantsev, Khorezm was released from the political and economic dependence of the Achaemenids at the end of the 5th century BC.[123]

Researcher K. Sobirov founded the independent state of Khorezm in Saksafar (519-517) from the end of the 5th century BC, his successors Farasman (329-320 BC), Khusrav (320 BC) ruled Amu Darya right and left. Those who built irrigation facilities in the regions and established agricultural culture in their regions, in turn, built castles on the heights connected to

---

[118] Массон В.М. Ромодин В.А. История Афганистане –М,: 1964. Т-1. –С 71.

[119] Дандамаев М. А Политическая история Ахеменидской державы. – М.: 1985. – С.248.

[120] Ставиский Б.Я. Средияя Азие в ахеменидскую эпоху/История Таджикистано народа Душанбе. 1998. Т. 1 – С. 270.

[121] Рапопорт Ю.А. Краткий очерк истории Хорезмской археолого – этнографической экспедиции. – М,:1998. – С.33.

[122] Вайнберг Б.И. Заключения // Калали-гыр-2. Культовый центр в Древнем Хоразме IV-II вв до.н.э. –М,: 2004 – С.237.

[123] Балахванцев А. С. Отделение Хорезма от государсива Ахеменидов// Хорезм в истории государственности Узбекистана – Ташкент,: 2013 – С.60.

the foot of the Amu Darya coast at the beginning, middle and end of the irrigation facilities.

One of the religious-ideological settlements built by the population on the right bank of the Amu Darya is the monument of Jonboskala in the fourth century BC, in the form of a rectangle, the total size of which is 3.5 hectares. In his first monograph, SP Tolstov restored the ancient state of Yonboshkala. Yanboshkala in its restored state is located in the south-west of the temple.[124]Yonboshkala was a religious-ideological center in antiquity and had the status of a state.

Koykirylgankala - was erected as a symbol of the sun in the 4th century BC and 4th century AD. It served as a religious-ideological center.[125]

Aqchakhankala is located in the territory of Beruni district, the total area is 55 ha. In the north-east of the monument, a palace and a temple where the "100 base" column has been preserved have been explored. In the middle of the inner center, there was a main fire station directed to four gates.[126]

Tashkhirmontepa is the capital city of the micro-oasis of Aqchakhankala cultural and economic center, and the fireplace in the house-room is intended for the faith of the people. The fire place was in the system of Aqchakhankala, the main temple.[127]

Ayozkala - 3. One of the monuments of the archaeological complex of Sultan Uwais Mountain, it was built

---

[124] Толстов С.П. Древний Хорезм. – М,: МГУ, 1948 – С 93. Рис 29 а

[125] Кой – крылган - кала – памятник культуры Древнего Хорезма IV в до. н. э. – IV. в. н. э // ТрХАЭЭ. Т.V – М,: Наука, 1967. – С. 307.

[126] Хўжаниёзов F.К. Қадимги Хоразм мудофаа иншоотлари – Тошкент, "Ўзбекистон", 2007 – Б. 43-44.

[127] Ягодин В.Н, Беттс. Г Ташкырмансоий древний оазис: Казакли – Ятган, Ташхирмантепе/ Тезисы докладов Международного симпозиума « Приаралье на перекрестке культури и второго полевого семинара « Археология древнего Тащкырмансково оазиса – Нукус – Бустан, 2007. – С 109-110.

by artisans and engineers in the IV century BC, and was the main city of the farming oasis until the IV century AD. In its southeast corner, a temple served as a place of religious faith.[128]

It is added to the Toqtov height on the north-west side of the Toqkala-Beruniy-Nukus road, with a total area of 8 ha. The monument functioned as a religious-ideological center from ancient times to the beginning of the 13th century.[129]

Tuproqkala - Ellikkala district in the 4th century BC in a rectangular shape on the plain, the total area is 17 ha. The city temple is located in the south-eastern corner and was active until the 9th century AD.[130]

Ayozkala - 2. It was built in a circular shape on the north-west side of the Ayozkala-1 monument in the II-I centuries BC. In its northern part, the remains of a temple were archaeologically studied. The monument continued as a religious-ideological center in the 9th century AD. The operation of the Amu Darya irrigation facility has ended due to the interruption of water supply.[131]

Religious and ideological centers in the Left Bank area:

Hazorasp - in the south of the Khorezm oasis, it was built by the population on the border of the nomadic world, and different opinions about which historical period it belongs to are observed in the works of researchers. For example, Y.Gulomov placed the monument in 1000 BC. V-IV centuries.[132]

In the publications of the Khorezm archeological-ethnological expedition, Y.G.Ghulomov's conclusion on the

---

[128] Собиров.Қ Хоразмнинг қишлоқ ва шаҳарлари мудофаа иншоотлари. – Тошкент, Фан, 2009 – Б 74-75.

[129] Гудкога А. В. Токкала – Ташкент, Фан, 1964 – С. 50-70.

[130] Городище Топрак-кала// ТрХАЭЭ, - М, Наука, 1981. Т.XII – С 146.

[131] Манылов Ю.П. Городище Аёзкала – 2 – Уникальный памятних раннесредневекого Харезма// Археология приаралья – Ташкент, Фан, 1984. С. 40-52

[132] Ғуломов Я. Ғ. Хоразмнинг суғорилиш тарихи-Тошкент; - Фан, 1959 – Б 87-88.

issue of the first construction of Hazarasp was supported.[133] A temple is located 100 m south of the gate in the middle of the eastern wall of the monument.

Ichankala (Khiva) was built as a military fortification at the end of the 5th century BC on the border of Karakum, with a total area of 26 hectares. The eastern part of the monument has a temple, which currently exists as an Islamic shrine with a wooden pillar.[134]

Jigarband - built on a hill connected to the foot of the left bank of the Amu Darya (until the beginning of the 13th century). Located on the international caravan route, it fulfilled a religious-ideological task.[135]

Tuproqkala (Shavot) - was built in the village of Manoq in the Shavot district of the Khorezm region, the total area of which was 4 ha in ancient times. The monument was built in the image of the sun and was a religious-ideological center until the early Middle Ages.[136]

Tashkala-2 Tuproqkala massif to the plain (region of the foot of the left bank of Amu Darya) in a square shape of 0.5 ha.

---

[133] Воробьева М.Б, Лариров – Скобло, Неразкин Е.Е. Археологические работы в Хазараспе в 1958-1959 гг. – М, 1963 – С. 165-167. Сабиров К, Абдиримов А Хазарасп и вопросы период изации ранних этанов развития осеро земледельческой культуры Харезме//Международный симпозиум «Цивилизация древнего Хорезма в контекете истории мировой культуры» и палевой семинар «Археология древнего Тащкырманнского оазисе»/Тезисы докладов и материалы к симпозиуму. Нукус – Бустон.2000 – С 35.

[134] Мамбетуллаев М, Ягодин В.Н. К оценке хронологии и исторической динамики культурного слие древней – Хивы // Ташкент,: - ОНУ, 1986. Вып 8. С. 43-51.

[135] Вишневская О.А. Раскопки городица Джигарбент//АО 1975 – М, Наука, 1976 – С.544.

[136] Собиров Қ. Хоразм шаҳарлари тарихи. – Қўлёзма, 2022 – Б 105.

BC It was built in the 4th century and served as a temple until the beginning of the 13th century.[137]

Kalalikir-2 is located in the north-western part of the Amudarya Davdon tributary in the Sarikamishboi basin. Sarmanyob was supplied with water by a spring from the irrigation system, and was a religious center of the population from the 4th century BC to the 4th century AD.[138]

Katkala is built on a plain connected to the foot of the Amu Darya left bank. It served as a religious-ideological center from the 4th century BC to the 9th century AD.[139]

Oyboyirkala is located on a height in the north-west of the Ustyurt plateau. It was built in the wrong square shape at the end of the 5th century - the beginning of the 4th century BC. The total area is 10 ha. The monument is located on the international caravan route. The religious faith of the inhabitants of the castle was carried out in a special temple.[140]

Katkala II - 24 km from the city of Urganch, Shavot district, located in the area of Katkala in an irregular rectangular shape, the total size is 8.5 ha. In the interior of the castle, a temple was built on the right side of the corridor leading straight from the gate.[141]

"Almaotishgan" - 1 - A circular building was built on the plain in the farmer's area of Avaz Utar, Yangariq district

---

[137] Баратов С. Матрасулов Ш. Археологические работы в южном Харезме/ Археологическиье иссредования в Узбекистане 2002 г – Самарканд, 2003 – С.Б.117.

[138] Калали – гыр-2. Культовый центр в древнем Харезме IV-II в.в до. н.э.// Опв вед. Б.И. Вайнберг – М, Вост мир 2004 – С. 6-11

[139] Маныров Ю.П. К изучению городица Кят//Вестник КК Ф Ан УзССР. – Нукус,: 1966 №2 – С .49-56.

[140] Мамбетуллаев М. Исследование храмового комплекса Большая Айбуйир-кала/ Археология Узбекистана – Ташкент, 2011.№1 –С.52-61.

[141] Мамбетуллаев М. Городище Кат/ Левобережнии и Зарлыкэшонбобо//Археологические исслодования в Каракалпакии- Ташкент:, Фан, 1981 – С.68-72.

(0.5 ha). Zoroastrian traditions were carried out and continued until the 4th century AD.[142]

Gaurkala - 3 - built in a triangular shape in the southern area of Gaurkir. It was a religious and worship center until the 4th century AD.[143]

Dargham (Darghan Ota) was added to the height connected to the foot of the Amu Darya coast. In ancient times, its area was 6 ha. The monument is located on the road of international caravan communication. It was a center of faith for residents and caravan participants.[144]

Great Urganch - the center of the village of Kokhna Urgench, present-day Tashovuz region. The total area is 400 ha, and the almshouse is located in the southeastern region. It is a city with state status.[145]

---

[142] Матрасулов Ш, Собиров Қ Олмаотишган ёдгорлигидаги археологик тадқиқотлар//Археологические исследования в Узбекистане в 2001г – Самарканд 2002 – Б. 104-107.

[143] Коляков С.М. Раскопки исодьбы Гауркала-3// АО 1984: - М, Наука 1985. Б 524-530.

[144] Юсупов Х. Путиводитель по археолого-архитектурной памятники Ташаузолой области – Ашхабад 1989 – С.21-22.

[145] Юсупов Х. Сердце древнего Хорезма – Ашхабад, - 1993 – С.20-21.

Summary

Our ancestors in the area between Tewarak and the surrounding desert sand dunes achieved a high material and spiritual culture in the development of all areas of the economy, using the available natural resources in a timely manner from the IV-III millennium BC. . The sernam and serunum plains, created as a result of the Amu Darya's gradual extraction of mineral substances from the water over the course of centuries, created a wide opportunity for our ancestors to develop various fields of crafts. Since the beginning of the world, the human being is gradually growing in the process of carrying out economic activities under the influence of the geographical environment, climatic conditions and ecology.

In the works of the Khorezm expedition, the late stone, Mesolithic and early Neolithic period (VI-V - the first half of the millennium) are objects that showed interest in the knowledge of jewelry in the spiritual world view of the people who lived in the foothills of the Sultan Uwais mountain of the geographical latitude of the lower Amu Darya basin. not recorded. In the course of the historical path of our ancestors in their daily activities, it is possible to study the ideas of adornment in their spirituality into two historical periods.

1. The historical period is from the IV - III millennium BC - the end of the II millennium BC;
2. Historical period 10th century BC - 4th century AD.

In the second half of the 5th millennium BC - the first half of the 4th millennium BC, the clan communities settled at the foot of the Sultan Uwais mountain settled in the regions of the Okchadarya basin, at the foot of the shores of the reservoirs in the vicinity of Yonboshkala, and invented several fields of economy. those who did. In other words, new branches of handicrafts have emerged, including the making of tools made of stone and bone, round beads from flint and square stones, the idea of decorating men and women has arisen due to the emergence of spiritual knowledge, which in turn has led to the idea of further improvement in the future. ignored in their daily activities. In this historical period, beads made of stone and bone were widely used in everyday activities. In our opinion, The use of beads was a great opportunity for the leader of the clan "wise mother". In the Eneolithic and Bronze Age, beads were made of stone, bone, and copper. In the Iron Age and Antiquity, jewelry beads were made from materials such as stone, bone, and copper.

From the fourth century BC, a new era began in the work of the oasis residents and in the art of jewelry. From this period, the handicrafts of the sedentary people who enjoyed the economic and military power of the centralized state developed exceptionally fine jewelry.

Beads, rings and bracelets of different colors and different functions from available natural resources gave unnatural ornaments to the neck, front chest, ears and fingers of our ancestors. Today, the history of jewelry used by our women, and in some cases by men, is connected to the jewelry that was the product of "life and creativity" of the clan communities of the Neolithic period.

List of used literature:

1. Архангельский. А. Д. Геологические исследования в низовьях Амударьи. Москва, 1931.
2. Афанасьев. А.Н Поэтические возрения славян на природы – М,:1965.
3. Андринов. Б. В. Древние оросительные системи Приаралья. М, «Наука», 1969.
4. Андрианов.Б.В. Земледелия наших предков. М, "Наука", 1978.
5. Антонова Е.В. Очерки культуры древних земледельцев Передней и Средней Азии. Опыт реконструкции мировосприятия М.: «Наука», 1984.
6. Авесто / Асқар Маҳкам таржимаси.
7. Авесто. Яшт китоби/М.Исхоков таржимаси. – Тошкент: "Шарк" 2001.
8. Анорбоева А, Исломов У, Матбобоев Б Ўзбекистон тарихида қадимги Фарғона-Тошкент, Фан, 2001.
9. Аширов. А.А. Ўзбек халқининг қадимги эътиқод ва маросимлари. 2001.
10. Аширов А.А. "Авесто"дан мерос маросимлар - Тошкент: "А. Кодирий номидаги Халк мероси" нашриёти, 2001.
11. Аскаров А Қадимги Хоразм тарихига оид баъзи бир масалалар//Ўзбекистон этнологияси: Янгича карашлар ва ёндашувлар – Тошкент, 2004.
12. Абдалов У.М. Хоразм воҳасининг қадимий диний эътиқод ва маросимлари зардуштийлик анъана ва маросимлари, Тошкент: "Yoshlar avlodi", 2021.
13. Берг. Л.С. Климат и жизнь. М, 1947.
14. Бижанов Е.Б. Виноградов А.В. Неолитические памятники Каракалпакского Устюрта//Вестник Каракалпакского филиала АН УЗ ССР-Нукус, 1965, №3.
15. Бижанов Е.Б. Новые данные о неолите юго-западногр Устюрта//Вестник Каракалпакского филиала АН Уз ССР. – Нукус, 1980.

16. Бижанов Е.Б. Мезолитические и неолитические памятники северо-западного Устюрта//Археология Приаралья. – Ташкент, Вып-1, 1982.
17. Бижанов Е.Б. Открытые памятники мезолита на юге-восточном Устюрте//Вестник Каракалпакского Филиала АН УЗССР. –Нукус, Вып-3, 1982.
18. Бижанов Е.Б. Первое неолитическое погребение на Устюрте. - СА, Наука, 1985.
19. Баратов. П. Ўзбекистон табиий – географияси. Тошкент, " Ўқитувчи", 1996.
20. Болелов С.Б Некоторые итор археологи чесних работ на Хумбузтепе// Ону, - Ташкент. 1999.
21. Баратов.П., М.Маматқулов., А.Рафиқов. Ўрта Осиё табиий географияси. Тошкент, " Ўқитувчи", 2002.
22. Баратов С. Матрасулов Ш. Археологические работы в южном Харезме/ Археологическиье иссредования в Узбекистане 2002 г – Самарканд, 2003.
23. Балахванцев А. С. Отделение Хорезма от государситва Ахеменидов// Хорезм в истории государственности Узбекистана – Ташкент,: 2013.
24. Воробьева М.Б, Лариров – Скобло, Неразкин Е.Е. Археологические работы в Хазараспе в 1958-1959 гг. – М, 1963.
25. Виноградов А.В. Неолитические памятники Хорезма. -МХЭ, М, Наука, 1968.
26. Воробъева М.Г. Дингильдже. Чадьба середины I тысячелетия до.н.7.в Древнем Хорезме//МХЭ, М,:1973.

27. Виноградов. А. В.,М.А.Итина, А.С.Кесь. Мамедов. Э.Д. Палеографическая обусловленность расселения древнего человека в пустыях Средней Азии//Первобытный человек, его материальная культура и природная среда в плейстоцене и голоцене//М, «Наука», 1974.
28. Виноградова А.В. Мамедов Э.Д. Ланшафтно-климатические условия среднеазиатских пустынь в голоцене//ИМКУ-Ташкент, 1974 №11.

29. Вишневская О.А. Раскопки городица Джигарбент//АО 1975 – М, Наука, 1976.
30. Винаградов А.В, Бижанов Е.Б. Первие палеолитические находки с юго – восточнова Устюрта/АО, 1977. –М, Наука, 1978.
31. Вайнберг Б.И. Памятники Куюсайской культуры //Кочевники на границах Хорезма//ТР. ХАЭЭ-М, Наука, - М 1979.
32. Виноградов А.В. Древние охотники и реболове Среднеазиатского междуречья.- М, Наука, 1981.
33. Вайнберг Б.И. Скобоворческие племени в древнем Хорезма – М.Наука, 1981
34. Виноградов А.В. Итина М, А, Яблонский Л.Т. Древнейшее население низавий Амударьи- М. Наука, 1986.
35. Вишневская О.А, Рапопорт Ю.А. Городшие Кюзели-гыр. К вопросу о раннеи этапы истории Хорезма//ВДИ – М,:1997,№2
36. Виноградова Е.А. Первие палеолитические находки в\ Султонуиздаге//Приаралье в древности и средневековье.-М, Наука, 1998.
37. Вайнберг.Б.И. Этногеография Турана в древности. М, «Наука», 1999.
38. Вайнберг Б.И. Заключения // Калали-гыр-2. Культовый центр в Древнем Хоразме IV-II вв до.н.э. –М,: 2004.
39. Геродот. IX. II.
40. Герасимов.И.И. Основные черты развития современной Турана//ТИГ.Вып.25//. 1937.
41. Герасимов.И.И. Марков.К.К. Четвертичная геология. Москва, 1939.
42. Ғуломов. Я. Ғ. Хоразмнинг суғорилиш тарихи. Тошкент, "Фан", 1959.
43. Гудкога А. В. Токкала – Ташкент, Фан, 1964.
44. Городище Топрак-кала(Раскопки 1965-1975г)//ТХЛЭЭ//. Т. Х11, М., Наука» 1981.

45. Герасимовский А.И. Древности Хивм и Амударьинского отдела. //Исторический вестник (XVII, сентябрь), 1909.
46. Ғ.Ходжаниязов. Қадимги Хоразм мудофаа иншоотлари. Тошкент, "O'ZBEKISTON", 2007.
47. Димо.Н.А. Почвенные исследования в бассейне в Амударьи// Ежеговник отдело земельных улучшений за 1913г. Ч.2, СПб, 1914.
48. Дандамаев М. А Политическая история Ахеменидской державы. – М.: 1985.
49. Жавлиев Т. Табиат, инсон ва дин. – Тошкент, Фан, 1986.
50. Жуманазаров У. Тарих, афсона ва дин – Тошкент,: Ўзбекистон, 1990.
51. Жўраев М Ўзбек халқ эътиқодларида сирли рақамлар – Тошкент: Фан, 1991.
52. Заднепровский Ю.А. Памятники Андроновской культуры. К вопросу о сувярганской культуре// Средняя Азия в эпоху камня и бронзы М-Л, Наука, 1966.
53. Иванин. М. И. Хива и река Амударьи. СПб, 1873, с. 37 – 39. Каульбарс. А. В. Низовья Амударьи, описание по собственным исследованниям в 1873г// ЗИРГО, Т. 3// СПб, 1881.
54. Итина М.А. Работы Узбойского отряда в 1957г//КСИЭ, М. Наука, 1958.
55. Итина М.А. Женская статуэтка элоль ранней бронза из Хорезм//КСИЭ- М: 1958
56. Итина М.А. История степных племен южного Приаралья //ТР ХАЭЭ-М, Наука, 1977.
57. Исламов У. Древнейшая перещерная палеолитическая стоянка Селенгур Ферганской долине – СА, 1990.
58. Искоков М. Авесто. Хуршед Яшт//Ўзбек тили ва адабиёти.-Ташкент,: 1999.
59. Исламов У. Фарғонанинг ибтидоий тарихи. Тошкент, Фан, 2001.

60. Исоқов З. Фарғона анъанавий дехқончилик маданияти Тошкент: "Янги нашр", 2011.
61. Йулдошев Н. Бухоро авлиёлари тарихи. – Бухоро: "Бухоро" нашриёти, 1997.
62. Кесь.А.С. Природные факторы, обусловающие расселение древнего человека в пустыне Средней Азии//КСИЭ, Вып ХХХ//. М, «Наука», 1958.
63. Кой – крылган - кала – памятник культуры Древнего Хорезма IV в до. н. э. – IV. в. н. э // ТрХАЭЭ. Т.V М,: Наука, 1967.
64. Касымов М,Р. Многослойная палеолитическая стоянка Кульбулак в Узбекистане-МИА, 185, М. 1972.
65. Кесь.А.С. Аральское море в голоцене//Археология и этнография Средней Азии//. Москва, «Наука», 1979.
66. Коляков С.М. Раскопки исодьбы Гауркала-3// АО 1984: - М, Наука 1985.
67. Кабиров Ж, Сагдуллаев А.С. Ўрта Осиё археологияси – Ташкент, : Ўқитувчи, 1990.
68. Қурбонниёзов.Р. Хоразм географияси. Урганч, 1996.
69. Калали – гыр-2. Культовый центр в древнем Харезме IV-II в.в до. н.э.// Опв вед. Б.И. Вайнберг – М, Вост мир 2004.
70. Лазаренко А.А, Ранов В.А. Новая палеолитическая стоянка Каратау-1 в Южном Таджикистане//Успехи среднеазиатской археологи – Л, Наука. Вып-3, 1975.
71. Массон В.М. Ромодин В.А. История Афганистане – М,: 1964.
72. Маныров Ю.П. К изучению городица Кят//Вестник КК Ф Ан УзССР. – Нукус,: 1966.
73. Мирсоатов М.Т. Древние шахты Учтута – Ташкент, Фан, 1972.
74. Мамбетуллаев М. Городище Кат/ Левобережнии и Зарлыкэшонбобо//Археологические исслодования в Каракалпакии- Ташкент:, Фан, 1981.
75. Манылов Ю.П. Городище Аёзкала – 2 – Уникальный памятних раннесредневекого Харезма// Археология приаралья – Ташкент, Фан, 1984.

76. Мамбетуллаев М, Ягодин В.Н. К оценке хронологии и исторической динамики культурного слие древней – Хивы // Ташкент,: - ОНУ, 1986.
77. Маҳмуд Саттор. Ўзбек удумлари Тошкент: Фан, 1993.
78. Матрасулов Ш, Собиров Қ Олмаотишган ёдгорлигидаги археологик тадқиқотлар//Археологические исследования в Узбекистане в 2001г – Самарканд 2002.
79. Мамбетуллаев М. Исследование храмового комплекса Большая Айбуйир-кала/ Археология Узбекистана – Ташкент, 2011.
80. Матякубов Х. Хоразм воҳаси бронза ва илк темир даври тарихи-Тошкент, 2017.
81. Неразик. Е. Е. Раскопки городища Топраккала/КСИА АН СССР//, №132, М.,1972.
82. Неразик. Е. Е. Раскопки городища Топраккала// АО 1974.-М. »Наука» 1975.
83. Нестеров А. Прошлое приаральских степей в преданиях киргиз Казалинского уезда. ЗВО. Т. XII. Вмп.ГУ. СПб, 1900.
84. Низовья Амударьи, Сарыкамыш, Узбой//История формирования и заселения//. МХЭ, Вып, №3,М, «Наука», 1960.
85. Полибий. Умумий тарих. X.
86. Пугаченкова Г.А. Материалы к истории Хорезмского зодчества. //МХЭ. Вьш. 7. М. 1963.
87. Пьянков.И.В. Хорасмии Гекатея Милетсково// ВДИ, №2.,М, «Наука», 1972.
88. Рапопорт Ю.А Хорезмийские астодоны//С7,- М.:1962.
89. Рапопорт Ю.А., Гертман А.Н. Работы на Топраккале //АО 1976//. М., «Наука» 1977.
90. Россикова А.Е. По Амударье от Петро-Александровска до Нукуса. Русский Вестник, август, 1902.
91. Рак И.В. Мифы древнего и раннесредневекового Ирана СПб, 1998.

92. Рапопорт Ю.А. Краткий очерк истории Хорезмской археолого – этнографической экспедиции. – М,:1998.
93. Ртвелади Э.В. Об определении ряда географических терминов. Авесты // "Авесто" китоби тарихимизнинг ва маънавиятимизнинг илк ёзма манбаи мавзусидаги илмий-амалий семинар материаллари. Тошкент, 2000.
94. Рахмонов Ф.Ш. Қашқадарё аҳолисининг зироатчиликка оид урф-одат ва маросимлари (XIX асрнинг охира - XX аср бошлари). Тарих фанлари номзоди учун ёзилган дисс... Тошкент, 2002.
95. Страбон. География. XI.
96. Сарианиди В.Ы. Культовые здания поселений анауской культуры//СА – М, 1962 №1-С. 44-47, Хлопик И.Ж. Геоисторская группа поселений эпохо энеолита.-М-Л.: Наука, 1964
97. Созонова М.В. Традиционное хозяйство узбеков Южного Хорезма. - Л.: «Наука», 1978.
98. Снесарев Г.П. Реликты домусульманских верований и обрядов у узбеков Хорезма.
99. Ставискый Б.Я. Средияя Азие в ахеменидскую эпоху/История Таджикистано народа Душанбе. 1998.
100. Сабиров К, Абдиримов А Хазарасп и вопросы период изации ранних этанов развития осеро земледельческой культуры Харезме//Международный симпозиум «Цивилизация древнего Хорезма в контекете истории мировой культуры» и палевой семинар «Археология древнего Тащкырманнского оазисе»/Тезисы докладов и материалы к симпозиуму. Нукус – Бустон.2000.
101. Собиров.Қ Хоразмнинг қишлоқ ва шаҳарлари мудофаа иншоотлари. – Тошкент, Фан, 2009.
102. Сагдуллаев А.С, Матякубов Х.К Проблеме происхождение глинобытно сырцовой архитектуры в Хоразме/Вестник Национарьнаго Университета Узбекистана. – Ташкент:,2013.
103. Собиров Қ. Хоразм шаҳарлари тарихи. – Қўлёзма, 2022.

104. Толстов С.П. Пережитки тотемизм и дуальной организатции у туркмен//ПИДО. -1935.

105. Толстов. С.П. Древнехорезмийские памятники в Каракалпакии (Предварительные итоги археологических работ ИИМК в 1938г//ВДИ, М, Наука, - М, 1939.

106. Толстов.С.П. Древний Хорезм.МГУ,1948.

107. Толстов. С. П. По следам древнехорезмийской цивилизации. - М-Л, 1948.

108. Толстов С.П. Древний Хорезм. По следам древних культур. М. 1951.

109. Толстов.С.П., Кесь.А.С. История первобытных поселений на протоках древних дельт Амударьи и Сырдары//Сборник статей для XVIII международного географического конгресса//. М – Л,1956.

110. Толстов.С.П. Работы Хорезмской археолого-этнографической экспедиции в 1948-1953//ГРХАЭЭ-М., Наука, 1958.

111. Толстов. С. П. По древним дельтам Окса и Яксарта. - М, Наука, 1962.

112. Толстов С.П. Қадимги Хоразм маданиятини излаб. – Тошкент, Фан, 1964.

113. Фрезер Дж Золотие веть – М,: Полиёиздей 1990.

114. Хўжаниёзев. Г. Оқшахон ёки тарихда минг йил жумбоқ бўлиб келган номаълум қалъа хақида//Жайхун, №1//.Нукус., 1998.

115. Хўжаниёзев. Г. Х., Ягодин. В.Н., Хелмс. С.У., Макларен. Б.К. Раскопки на Ақшаханкалы//Археологические исследования в Узбекистане в 2001г//. Самарканд, 2000., Хожаниёзев. Г. Х., Хелмс. С.У., Снеддон. Э. Археологические исследования на городе Ақшаханкала в 2001 году//Археологические исследования в Узбекистане в 2001г//. Самарканд, 2002.

116. Хўжаниёзов Ғ.К. Қадимги Хоразм мудофаа иншоотлари – Тошкент, "Ўзбекистон", 2007.

117. Холматов. Н.Ў. Ўзбекистон неолит даври жамоалари моддий маданияти. - Тошкент, Фан, 2008.

118. Холматов. Н. Оқчадарё ҳавзаси неолит даври хусусида//Хоразм тарихи. Замонавий тадқиқотларда.- Тошкент-Урганч, Наврўз, 2019.

119. Шишкин В.А. Варахша. - М.: Изд-во Академии наук СССР, 1963.

120. Шаниязов К. К этнический истории узбекского народа...

121. Шайдуллаев Ш.Б, Шайдуллаев А.Ш. "Хоразм" атамасининг пайдо бўлиши ва семантикаси//Хоразм тарихи. Замонавий тадқиқотлар. –Тошкент-Урганч. Наврўз, 2019.

122. Ягодин. В. Н., Ходжаниязов. Г. Х., Статов. В. А. Внешняя стена городища Казаклы-Яткан// Ўзбекистон тарихи моддий ва ёзма манбаларда//. Т., "Фан", 2005.

123. Ягодин В.Н, Беттс. Г Ташкырмансоий древний оазис: Казакли – Ятган, Ташхирмантепе/ Тезисы докладов Международного симпозиума « Приаралье на перекрестке культури и второго полевого семинара « Археология древнего Тащкырмансково оазиса – Нукус – Бустан, 2007.

124. Юсупов Х. Путиводитель по археолого-архитектурной памятники Ташаузолой области – Ашхабад 1989.

125. Юсупов Х. Сердце древнего Хорезма – Ашхабад, - 1993.

LIST OF CONDITIONAL ABBREVIATIONS

АН- Академия наук

ВДИ - Вестник древней истории, Москва ИВЛ - Издательство восточной литературы, Москва

ИМКУ - История материальной культуры Узбекистана, Ташкент

КСИА- Краткие сообщения Института археологии, Москва

КСИЭ-Краткие сообщения Института этнографин, Москва

Л - Ленинград М-Москва

МГУ- Московский государственный университет

МИА - Материалы и исследования по археологии СССР. Москва, Ленинград

МХЭ- Материалы Хорезмской экспедиции, Москва

СА - Советская археология, Москва

ХАЭЭ - Хорезмская археолого-этнографическая экспедиция

ЮТАКЭ Южно-Туркменистанская археологическая комплексная экспедиция

APPLICATIONS

Aqchakhanqala murals

Earthen castle

Guldursinkala

Kirghizkala

Called fortress